Caring for a Child who has been Sexually Exploited

Eileen Fursland

coramBAAF
ADOPTION & FOSTERING ACADEMY

Published by
CoramBAAF Adoption and Fostering Academy
41 Brunswick Square
London WC1N 1AZ
www.corambaaf.org.uk

Coram Academy Limited, registered as a company limited by guarantee in
England and Wales number 9697712, part of the Coram group, charity number
312278

British Library Cataloguing in Publication Data
A catalogue record for this book is available from the British Library

ISBN 978 1 910039 65 6

Project management by Shaila Shah, Director of Publications, CoramBAAF
Designed by Helen Joubert Design
Printed in Great Britain by The Lavenham Press

Trade distribution by Turnaround Publisher Services, Unit 3, Olympia Trading
Estate, Coburg Road, London N22 6TZ

Contents

Acknowledgements

Our thanks go to everyone who has contributed to this book or whose experiences, knowledge and research we have been able to include in it as useful resources for those who want to understand more about child sexual exploitation and how to support young people to recover from it.

Thanks to Dr Lucie Shuker of the University of Bedfordshire's International Centre: Researching Child Sexual Exploitation, Violence and Trafficking and to Fiona Darlington Black for their input and for commenting on the draft. Thanks also to Lisa Weintrobe, CoramBAAF's Information Officer, who supplied information about the law in different parts of the UK. Stuart Hannah, child and adolescent psychotherapist, provided helpful input. We are also grateful to the many other individuals and organisations whose inquiries, research and work in this area have informed this book. These include Dr Shuker, Dr Carlene Firmin and their colleagues from the International Centre: Researching Child Sexual Exploitation, Violence and Trafficking; Barnardo's Safe and Sound Group; The Blast Project; and PACE UK. Their work with young people who have been sexually exploited must be challenging and at times heartbreaking, but it is making young victims' voices heard and changing the way society and agencies support them and tackle this crime. PACE UK has made a significant contribution to our understanding of the impact on parents and carers and it does invaluable work to ensure that they have the information they need and to support them through the darkest times.

I would like to express my gratitude to CoramBAAF for publishing *Caring for a Child who has been Sexually Exploited* and, in particular, Shaila Shah for commissioning and editing it.

Finally, to the foster carers and other care workers who we hope will read this book, we greatly respect you for the vital and life-changing work you are undertaking.

About the author

Eileen Fursland is a freelance writer specialising in issues affecting children and young people. She has written extensively for BAAF (now CoramBAAF) on a number of publications since 2002, as well as for a range of magazines and national newspapers and other organisations.

Eileen's publications for BAAF include the training course *Preparing to Adopt* (she wrote the first edition in 2002 with a working party from BAAF which devised the course, and the fourth edition, 2014, with Nicky Probert and Elaine Dibben); her books *Facing up to Facebook* (second edition 2013); *Social Networking and Contact* (2010); *Foster Care and Social Networking* (2011); *Social Networking and You* (2011); and *Ten Top Tips on Supporting Education*, with Kate Cairns and Chris Stanway. In earlier collaborations with Kate Cairns, she co-wrote BAAF's training programmes: *Trauma and Recovery*; *Safer Caring*; *Building Identity*; and *Transitions and Endings*.

Introduction

Child sexual exploitation can take many forms. Girls are groomed to believe that they are in a loving relationship – until the "boyfriend" starts to demand that she has sex with his friends and associates. Boys are being trapped in situations where they are being forced to have sex with many men, and threatened and attacked if they try to get out. Both girls and boys are sexually abused by other young people in street gangs. In many cases, child sexual exploitation (CSE) involves serious violence and in some cases, it also involves trafficking of several children or young people by organised groups of older men. Almost all cases of CSE involve online contact of one kind or another; it's clear that social networking provides an easy way for perpetrators both to make contact with young people and to exert control over them with threats and intimidation.

The various inquiries and reports that have been, and are being, undertaken in recent years have shone a spotlight on different types of child sexual exploitation and the way that many young victims have been badly let down by the agencies and services that should be protecting them. In some cases the response of local authorities and police has been appalling: the Jay inquiry (Jay, 2014) into child sexual exploitation in Rotherham between 1997 and 2013, for example, showed that the police, the local council and other professionals either did not believe what they were told, did not see it as abuse or felt unable to do anything about it. Victims asked for help and, shamefully, this was denied them. In the past, too many victims have been blamed and seen as promiscuous or even as "child prostitutes" – with tragic results.

There are still some people who do not understand the complex nature of CSE and the methods used to manipulate young victims, and who somehow see victims as having consciously chosen this path. But thankfully, much has been learned in the last few years about CSE. Our knowledge and understanding of the nature of CSE, and how perpetrators operate, are developing and attitudes are changing. Society as a whole is recognising that child sexual exploitation is an abhorrent crime that wrecks young lives.

A growing national priority

CSE is a growing national priority. Combating it involves agencies working together to identify victims, prosecute perpetrators and disrupt their activities wherever possible, support victims to help them recover, and to work on early prevention. It should also involve addressing wider social beliefs and cultures that can make it harder for us to see this form of abuse.

CSE can be classed as a particular type of sexual violence towards young people; in turn, sexual violence towards young people takes place in a broader context of societal sexual violence and gender inequality (Beckett *et al*, 2013).

Many practitioners are now exploring and developing new ways of working with young people and tackling this threat to their wellbeing, and there are many examples of good practice in services and projects.

Working with parents and carers

It is becoming clear from both working practice and academic research that working with parents and carers is crucial for both preventing and responding to CSE. The existing model of child protection was designed primarily to counter child abuse within the home, with the focus being on the parents and their behaviour. However, in child sexual exploitation the child or young person is the victim of an abuser who is usually from *outside the family*. In most cases, parents and carers are desperate to protect their child, while perpetrators drive a wedge between them and their child. So a new model is needed to respond to the specific emotional and relational dynamics of this situation and its impact on the family. In this "relational safeguarding model" (PACE UK, 2014), professionals work in partnership with parents and carers, supporting them to safeguard their child and increasing the chance of successfully prosecuting perpetrators.

Some children are already in care when they are exploited, so carers need to know how to spot the signs that they are at risk. However, a number of older children and young people are taken into care for their own safety, to remove them from the individuals and gangs perpetrating the CSE. In a few cases, for instance where there have been threats to families to intimidate them from giving evidence in court, victims are relocated together with their families.

There is debate about which form of care might be most appropriate and whether placing victims in foster placements or residential children's homes or secure units is the best way to respond to CSE. Ideally, all victims should be able to stay in their homes with their families, who would be supported to protect them, while the perpetrators would be the ones removed from the scene. Relocating a victim – because you can't keep them safe where they are – can potentially undermine them in other ways, disrupting some of their more positive relationships. And of course they cannot stay in the placement for ever.

There is a growing feeling that professionals and practitioners should try to avoid individualising CSE; they should focus less on the behaviour of individual children (for example, when young people are described as "putting themselves at risk") and more on the links between CSE victims and perpetrators locally, the context(s) in which it occurs, and how CSE can be disrupted and prevented and the perpetrators convicted. This approach is known as "contextual safeguarding".

In its latest guidance (Department for Education (DfE), 2017), the Government has said that agencies should move beyond a reactive approach (one that removes the individual from harm) to one that also addresses the existence of harm and/or proactively prevents that harm.

For the time being, however, it is still often the case that a child or young person is removed from the situation in order to keep them safe from their abuser(s) or because they are going missing and CSE is suspected. They are placed in foster care or a residential placement (sometimes far from home) or, in some cases, with a kinship carer or guardian. That means carers having to take on the challenging task of looking after a vulnerable child or young person who has been enticed, seduced, manipulated, threatened, degraded, hurt and terrified by their abusers.

If you are a parent, guardian, kinship carer or foster carer of a child or young person who has been sexually exploited, or if you work with such young people in a residential care setting, this book is for you.

The huge challenge facing anyone who is looking after a child – whether in a personal or professional role – who has been a victim of CSE is to show them that someone *does* care and that something *can* be done to turn things around.

But can you form a protective relationship with a child who has experienced things that no child ever should? Often they won't thank you for your care and concern – at least, not right away. Some young people don't perceive themselves to be a victim, don't want any intervention and reject attempts to help them – or are afraid of what their abuser might do to them if agencies get involved. They may be hostile to anyone who tries to help them get away from their abuser. Others are traumatised and terrified, convinced that no-one can protect them or help them.

Understanding what CSE is and how perpetrators groom, manipulate and intimidate their victims will enable you to better understand and support a child or young person who is experiencing it or has experienced it.

We hope this book will increase your understanding of CSE and responses to it, and that it will help you in the vital work of supporting the child in your care to stay safe, recover from their traumatic experiences, and start to rebuild their life.

What this book will cover (and what it won't)

Child sexual exploitation is a specific type of child sexual abuse (see below).

This book does not set out to cover every kind of child abuse and exploitation (though some of the information will be applicable in all situations).

We have included:

- CSE by individuals, organised groups and gangs (it can involve members of the family – though that is more rare, e.g. a mother who sells her daughter);

- CSE that occurs online.

We have not included:

- Child sexual abuse which is outside the definition of CSE, for example, sexual abuse by an adult where no "exchange" or "transaction" features and where the adult's motivation is sexual gratification alone. This would include most cases of child abuse by adults in, for example, schools, residential institutions, sports, the church and youth organisations. Where this has occurred or is suspected, the police and/or children's services should of course be informed (see Useful Organisations);

- Child sexual abuse within the child's family (i.e. by members of the family or extended family);

- The sexual exploitation of children and young people trafficked into the UK from overseas (but see page 22)

- Exploitation of young people that does not involve any kind of sexual activity (e.g. forced labour).

1 Child sexual exploitation: what it is and how the perpetrators operate

What is child sexual exploitation?

This is the latest definition and guidance from the Government:

> Child sexual exploitation is a form of child sexual abuse. It occurs where an individual or group takes advantage of an imbalance of power to coerce, manipulate or deceive a child or young person under the age of 18 into sexual activity (a) in exchange for something the victim needs or wants, and/or (b) for the financial advantage or increased status of the perpetrator or facilitator. The victim may have been sexually exploited even if the sexual activity appears consensual. Child sexual exploitation does not always involve physical contact; it can also occur through the use of technology.

> Like all forms of child sexual abuse, child sexual exploitation:

- can affect any child or young person (male or female) under the age of 18 years, including 16- and 17-year-olds who can legally consent to have sex;

- can still be abuse even if the sexual activity appears consensual;

- can include both contact (penetrative and non-penetrative acts) and non-contact sexual activity;

- can take place in person or via technology, or a combination of both;

- can involve force and/or enticement-based methods of compliance and may, or may not, be accompanied by violence or threats of violence;

- may occur without the child or young person's immediate knowledge (through others copying videos or images they have created and posting on social media, for example);

- can be perpetrated by individuals or groups, males or females, and children or adults. The abuse can be a one-off occurrence or a series of incidents over time, and range from opportunistic to complex organised abuse; and

- is typified by some form of power imbalance in favour of those perpetrating the abuse. Whilst age may be the most obvious, this power imbalance can also be due to a range of other factors including gender, sexual identity, cognitive ability, physical strength, status, and access to economic or other resources.

...Even where a young person is old enough to legally consent to sexual activity, the law states that consent is only valid where they make a choice and have the freedom and capacity to make that choice. If a child feels they have no other meaningful choice, are under the influence of harmful substances, or fearful of what might happen if they don't comply (all of which are common features in cases of child sexual exploitation), consent cannot legally be given whatever the age of the child.

Child sexual exploitation is never the victim's fault, even if there is some form of exchange: all children and young people under the age of 18 have a right to be safe and should be protected from harm. One of the key factors found in most cases of child sexual exploitation is the presence of some form of exchange (sexual activity in return for something) for the victim and/or perpetrator or facilitator.

Where it is the victim who is offered, promised or given something they need or want, the exchange can include both tangible (such as money, drugs or alcohol) and intangible rewards (such as status, protection or perceived receipt of love or affection). It is critical to remember the unequal power dynamic within which this exchange occurs and to remember that the receipt of something by a child/young person does not make them any less of a victim. It is also important to note that the prevention of something negative can also fulfil the requirement for exchange, for example, a child who engages in sexual activity to stop someone carrying out a threat to harm his/her family.

Whilst there can be gifts or treats involved in other forms of sexual abuse (e.g. a father who sexually abuses but also buys the child toys), it is most likely referred to as child sexual exploitation if the "exchange", as the core dynamic at play, results in financial gain for, or enhanced status of, the perpetrator.

Where the gain is only for the perpetrator/facilitator, there is most likely a financial gain (money, discharge of a debt or free/discounted goods or services) or increased status as a result of the abuse.

If sexual gratification, or exercise of power and control, is the only gain for the perpetrator (and there is no gain for the child/young person) this would not normally constitute child sexual exploitation, but should be responded to as a different form of child sexual abuse. (DfE, 2017, pp5–6)

The final paragraph (deliberately italicised) indicates that the Government excludes certain types of child abuse that would still be considered by many people to constitute child sexual exploitation. Sometimes the term "child sexual exploitation" is wrongly used to describe *any* situation where children are sexually abused during adolescence. The power imbalance, exchange or transactions are the key features. Clearly, it is impossible to be clear about the motivations and "gains" of perpetrators – or indeed victims – in every case.

Children may appear or claim to be exercising "choice" but sometimes they are not making choices freely. They may feel they have no other option but to comply because, for example, the perpetrator is offering something they badly need or is threatening or blackmailing them.

CSE is not just about the offence but about the context and situation in which it occurs.

For example, a homeless 17-year-old may "choose" to exchange sex for a place to stay, rather than sleep on the streets. A 14-year-old may "choose" to exchange sex for drugs because using drugs is the only way they can cope with the memories of previous abuse. A 16-year-old may "choose" to leave a placement (where they are physically safe) and get in a car with several men who they suspect are going to rape them, as they have been told if they don't, their younger sibling will be raped. All can be argued to be "making choices", but all are doing so from a position of vulnerability, fear or need. None is making an "active lifestyle choice" or is any less a victim because of that "choice".

Understanding the context within which "choices" are made is critical to our ability to respond effectively to child sexual exploitation.

(Beckett *et al*, 2017)

Grooming

Abusers are not abusive right away. Often children and young people who are sexually exploited have first been subject to a process of grooming. The abuser targets a child and befriends them, making them believe that he (or she) can be trusted and lowering their inhibitions, then goes on to engage in sexual activity with them or persuade them to do things such as provide photos of themselves naked or film themselves performing sexual acts.

Where is the "exchange"? Some of the child's needs for attention, affection and love may be being met by the perpetrator (at least in the early stage). Or the child may be deriving some kind of more tangible benefit such as money or drugs. But slowly their choices are taken away. The initial "good times" turn bad and they end up in a situation where they feel they have no choice. It may be the perpetrator who is gaining, rather than the child.

Even though a young person may – on the surface, or initially – appear to be a willing partner, we need to recognise that this still constitutes child sexual exploitation.

> We must champion young people's rights and challenge assumptions that the young person is "consenting".

> (Lisa Thornhill, Lucy Faithfull Foundation, speaking at the *Children & Young People Now* conference *Tackling Child Sexual Exploitation: Prevention and Protection*, December 2016)

The story of Ellie, who was given support by a Derby-based charity called Safe and Sound, shows how she was groomed by men who took advantage of her age and vulnerability from a young age.

> I was missing a lot of school, things weren't great at home either and I started hanging around the streets with a friend.

> Cars would drive past us and beep. The men inside, who were always older, would shout that we were sexy and beautiful. We started hanging around the streets at night too.

> One day we met a man who must have been about 30 and I started seeing him. He was nice to me, I would see him every day. He invited us to his friend's house where we would drink alcohol and listen to music.

> I would stay out all night. Once we were on our own in the bedroom and he was touching me and I just let him do it. I just thought it was normal.

When I was 13 I was sitting on some steps outside with my friend, it was quite late, it was cold and two older men pulled up.

They asked us to get in the car and said they would get us more alcohol so we agreed. Then they parked in a car park and I got in the back seat with one of the men while my friend was in the front with the other.

He was pouring vodka into a coke bottle for me and then he started touching me. I didn't understand what was going on but I let him carry on as he'd been so nice to me. Now I know it was sexual assault.

Me and my friend were meeting different, older men every night.

I was kicked out of school and lost the support of a teacher who I'd been close to. One night we ended up in a man's flat and he said to my friend to come into the bedroom. The door was blocked by a settee and I went into the room where my friend was and she was being raped. She got dressed and ran past me and we managed to get out.

...Later, another man came into my life, he was older than me and at first it began with buying me drink and letting me stay in his flat. He would touch me but I didn't like him like that. He forced himself on me, I wasn't ready, I was 15. He raped me and did it more than once.

I don't think all this stopped until I was 17. I was depressed and on medication and I just stayed at home. I didn't disclose anything and never went into detail.

Now I'm so much more confident thanks to Safe and Sound. When I was in that relationship they told me that I was better than that. I was meeting with someone from Safe and Sound once a week and they were telling me this each time I saw them so it started sinking in. It was drummed into me.

They would tell me about what was happening to me and what should be happening to me.

Now I'm moving on and I'm out of CSE. I know I don't want that life any more. I have learnt from what happened to me and now it fuels my future.

I loved coming to Safe and Sound and I really don't want to think about what my life would be like now if I hadn't been able to get help.

(http://safeandsoundgroup.org.uk/help-support/young-people/ellies-story/)

How do the offenders find and groom their victims?

Perpetrators use different methods to find their victims – sometimes they pick them up on the street (which happened to Ellie in the account above), and this is described in more detail below.

Researchers from the Security and Crime Science Doctoral Training Centre, University College London (UCL), and the Jill Dando Institute of Crime Science, UCL, London, carried out a study on "crime scripting", looking at the sequence of events involved in two cases of internal child sex trafficking that were investigated in UK police operations – see below. Their findings throw light on the methods used by offenders in these operations to target and groom their victims. (These cases involved girls, which is why victims are referred to as female in the section below.)

Starting points

Cruise

The offender looks for a new girl to abuse. Most offenders drove round looking for girls near schools, shopping centres, parks, under-18 discos, and other "target-rich" environments. Those who had no access to cars did this on foot.

Although some offenders were skilled in psychological manipulation, even for them it appears to have been a numbers game: approach enough girls and some will cave in...

Once identified, offenders relied on unsophisticated but effective tricks to get a girl's attention, such as whistling or shouting. They then bantered, flirted, or pestered their way to extracting name, age and telephone number.

Convert

The offender targets a girl who he, or a co-offender, already knows. Offenders regularly shared girls' phone numbers with each other, so many girls were called by complete strangers who knew their name, age and contact details.

Some girls passed on their friends' details to gratify or placate offenders and/or divert attention away from themselves.

Recruit via girl

This tactic involved recruiting new girls via existing victims. Some victims were regularly abused by men they perceived as their "boyfriends". These girls played an important role in bringing their own friends to abuse situations.

Re-abuse

Many girls were re-abused on at least one further occasion and a small number were abused by many men over a long period.

Pimp

Most abuse seemed to be motivated by non-commercial reasons, but some girls were pimped out to clients. Girls were pimped for money but may also have been exchanged for other commodities, used as a "sweetener" in drug deals or used to repay debts.

The grooming stage

The researchers found that once an abuser had found a victim by one means or another, they tended to use a range of tactics, often switching abruptly between them, for example, being nice one moment and nasty the next; there was no fixed grooming period, with offenders abusing some girls within minutes and grooming others for weeks.

It was common...for an offender to call the same girl repeatedly to break down initial resistance to meeting up. After what could be dozens of calls over a short period, many girls decided it was easier to pick up and agree to meet than face continuing bombardment.

The table below shows the range of behaviours that offenders used to groom victims:

Impact of behaviour and example(s) of behaviour

Flatter girl
Compliment girl
Flirt with girl
Explicitly treat girl as a "grown-up"
Profess to love girl

Build trust
Position oneself as a "friend" or "boyfriend" figure

Offer to help girl resolve any problems she may have
Give girl food or cigarettes
Protect girl from advances of other men in the group

Normalise sexual activity
Make sexually explicit jokes
Ask girl about her sexual experience and sexual preferences
Repeatedly talk about sex
Expose girl to pornographic material

Isolate girl
Insult or undermine friends, family or other support networks
Take girl to unfamiliar or difficult to access places
Separate girl from her friends if they are also present
Lock door and block girl's exit

Disorientate girl
Give girl alcohol and/or drugs
Spike girl's drink
Switch abruptly between nice and nasty behaviour
Speak in a language girl cannot understand

Intimidate girl
Make threats to hurt girl
Make threats to harm girl's family
Hit, slap or push girl
Laugh at or insult girl

Stage 3 was the abuse stage, which offenders moved into once they believed the girls were suitably groomed.

They invited targets to socialise, often offering to pick them up by car. They took girls to abuse locations, which were usually co-offenders' properties, cheap hotels, playing fields, or even parked cars in isolated areas...Offenders used various physical and non-physical isolation tactics. They locked doors or took away mobile telephones. Even if girls were not physically restrained, they may have been too afraid of repercussions, or disorientated due to drink, drugs, or an unfamiliar location to risk an escape attempt.

Abuse covered vaginal, oral, and anal rape, forced masturbation, and sexually inappropriate touching. In some cases it was not limited to a single action, but featured a number of offenders taking turns to abuse the victim. Offenders sometimes filmed abuse on mobile telephones and used it to scare other girls and presumably to brag to co-offenders. Once finished with a girl, offenders drove her home, arranged a taxi, or ordered her to leave. In a small number of cases, victims managed to escape. Varying levels of violence, pressure, and coercion often accompanied the abuse and deterred reporting.

(Reproduced from Brayley *et al*, 2011)

The changing "models" of CSE

Different types or models of child sexual exploitation occurring in various contexts, involving different ways of exerting control over victims, have been identified. Some of these are outlined below.

Grooming methods evolve and change and new models emerge as perpetrators find new ways to target victims and attempt to avoid detection and prosecution. For instance the "party-lifestyle" model is a relatively new method (see below).

Peer-to-peer abuse

CSE is just one form of peer-to-peer abuse. Peer-to-peer abuse includes sexual bullying, harassment, teenage relationship abuse, harmful sexual behaviour and (in 16- and 17-year-olds) domestic abuse. Within this, there will also be cases of child sexual exploitation where both the victim and the offender are aged under 18. It is important to note that professionals working in this complex area would not consider it appropriate to use the term "perpetrator" to refer to a young person under 18 who is abusing another young person. Young people who are abusing their peers need to be dealt with differently from adult offenders. In some cases they themselves are acting under duress from others.

Peer-to-peer abuse is happening in many contexts: in schools, on the streets, in flats and houses, in parks and disused garages, as well as – of course – in online spaces.

A young person can be simultaneously an offender (abusing another young person) and a victim themselves.

The abuse of children is often constructed around an age differential between the abuser and the abused, but in cases of peer-on-peer abuse this may not be the case. In such circumstances power imbalances can manifest in other ways sometimes related to gender, in other cases social status within peer groups, intellectual ability, economic wealth, social marginalisation and so on.

It is also important to note that while young people who abuse their peers have power over the young person they are harming, they may be simultaneously powerless in relation to some peers who are encouraging their behaviour or in the home where they are being abused. As children themselves we have to recognise the risk they pose to others as well as the risk they may face, and resist the urge to apply rigid victim/perpetrator divides that may not accurately reflect young people's experiences or our responsibilities towards them.

(Firmin and Curtis, 2015)

CSE can also be gang-related. This may involve young people abusing one another but it can also involve adults abusing young people. The Office of the Children's Commissioner carried out an Inquiry into Child Sexual Exploitation in Gangs and Groups (Berelowitz *et al*, 2013), and the findings published in the final report in 2013 were shocking.

Gang models of CSE can include gang initiation rituals, gang pressures and punishments.

The Inquiry's definitions of gangs and groups were as follows:

Gangs are relatively durable, predominantly street-based, social groups of children, young people and, not infrequently, young adults who see themselves, and are seen by others, as affiliates of a discrete, named group who:

- engage in a range of criminal activity and violence;
- identify or lay claim to territory;
- have some form of identifying structural feature; and
- are in conflict with similar groups

Groups are two or more people of any age, connected through formal or informal associations or networks including, but not exclusive to, friendship groups.

The interim report of the Inquiry, published in November 2012, revealed some findings about how perpetrators operate in the context of gangs and groups:

> *...control is exerted over victims in many different ways including threats of reprisals; violence; terrorising, victimising, corrupting, isolating, filling them with a fear of not being believed if they report what is happening to them; grooming; and coercion.*

They add:

> *We noted the methodical, devious and violent ways used by perpetrators to control children and young people and do with them what they wished.*

(Berelowitz *et al*, 2012)

As well as being groomed for crime and for drug-running, young people may also be forced to take part in harmful sexual behaviour against others.

Online grooming and CSE

Social networking has provided another way for perpetrators to find and groom young people (both girls and boys) and to sexually exploit them. It can be easier for perpetrators to contact and target their victims online rather than on the streets, and this type of grooming is becoming increasingly common. Some perpetrators are highly sophisticated and have a strategy, typically contacting large numbers of young people online, knowing that most won't respond but that a small number will. Others are simply opportunistic.

Online predators engage young people in conversation and subsequently attempt to incite them to strip or carry out sexual acts online or to meet in real life.

While using social networking, chat rooms or dating sites or playing online games, children can potentially start talking to strangers from anywhere in the world. Some children and young people respond to online approaches or accept "friend" requests indiscriminately.

In 2016, Barnardo's carried out a survey on online grooming. When grooming takes place online, the different stages – targeting, friendship-forming, loving relationship and abusive relationship – also apply. But, as the report points out:

> *These stages can progress very quickly online and not all stages, such as the loving relationship, may take place.*

(Fox and Kalkan, 2016)

The survey looked at five Barnardo's sexual exploitation services across the UK. In the previous six months, these five services alone had supported 702 children, and 42 per cent of the children had been groomed online. Of those groomed online, 61 per cent met the perpetrator and were sexually exploited. Almost half of those groomed online were also exploited by more than one offender – this included instances where children are groomed online and go on to meet the person who groomed them and be sexually exploited by them and others. Most of the children groomed online were between the ages of 14 and 17, though some victims were as young as 10 years old.

Below is a case example from one of Barnardo's services:

Josie, aged 12, has mild learning difficulties and autism. She loved a particular series of films, on which she was fixated. She was approached by a 28-year-old man on Facebook who claimed to be one of the characters from the movie. He got her to send indecent images of herself and he reciprocated by sending naked images of himself. In her mind they were in a relationship and she loved him and he loved her.

(Fox and Kalkan, 2016)

Perpetrators operate by initially seeming friendly, making flattering comments and making their victim feel "special". Very soon they will turn the conversation to sex, perhaps telling the victim he/she is sexy, asking about their sexual experience, asking for photos or suggesting talking via the webcam. They may encourage the child to engage in sexual role play, persuade them to undress, to pose in a sexually explicit way or to perform sexual acts on themselves in front of the webcam. Subsequently, they threaten to use the photos or videos to blackmail their victim into more and more explicit sexual behaviour or to meet in real life. They may threaten to expose the victim's photos or videos and send them to their parents or school friends. This causes untold mental anguish and fear for the victim. Tragically, some young people have committed suicide after being targeted in this way.

In 2011, Jake Ormerod, 20, of Torquay, Devon, was jailed for 10 years for sexual assault on a child and sexual activity with children. His offences related to eight girls as young as 13 and were committed over a three-year period. He had met the girls through Facebook and police said he was part of a paedophile gang who used the social networking site to target victims. The victims believed that Ormerod was their boyfriend. During the case, the court heard that lives had been shattered and childhoods destroyed and one of the victims had attempted suicide.

There have been cases of murder following online grooming and abuse but these are, of course, rare. In 2014, 14-year-old Breck Bednar was murdered by 19-year-old Lewis Daynes, whom he had met in an online gaming forum while playing war games like "Call of Duty". Daynes had befriended Breck and other adolescents in the online community. Over a period of months, he manipulated Breck, turning him against his family, giving him a mobile phone, and instructing him on lies to tell his family so that he could meet Daynes in his Essex flat.

Kayleigh Haywood from Measham, Leicestershire, was murdered in November 2015 after being groomed online. She had been chatting with a man on Facebook for two weeks before she was killed; they swapped mobile numbers and exchanged 2,600 messages. *Kayleigh's Love Story* is a five-minute video made as a warning by the police, who showed it to 35,000 secondary school pupils in the county in 2016. Following the screenings, 35 children made disclosures that they too had been groomed online.

It is often assumed that CSE occurring in an online context involves a perpetrator who is an older man pretending to be a teenager. However, this is by no means always the case. In some cases, the perpetrator is also relatively young, like Ormerod and Daynes. In other cases, some young people respond to approaches while being well aware that the person they are chatting to is much older. Some young people are very willing to engage with strangers online, and online chat can become sexual very quickly. The disinhibiting effect of online communication is well known and it is easy for young people to be seduced and flattered by online comments and to be drawn into responding in a sexual way.

Grooming and control by perpetrators using mobile phones

Sometimes the process of grooming can involve exchanging hundreds or thousands of text messages.

As well as perpetrators who target and groom their victims online, those who have met their victims in other ways commonly communicate with them via mobile phones, including texting and messaging, to control their behaviour, make threats, demand explicit photos or video, or to issue instructions, for example, about meeting or about recruiting other young people. In some cases, perpetrators use their phones to film victims being raped and abused.

If you are caring for a child or young person who has been a victim (or is suspected of having been a victim) of CSE, you will want to keep a close eye on their phone use so you know who is contacting them and whom they are contacting (see Chapter 6). Be aware that perpetrators often give their victims mobile phones in order to contact them more easily or to evade any monitoring by the victim's parents or carers.

Organised/network model and trafficking

The issue of child sexual exploitation began to come to light from around 2009 onwards as a result of high profile cases that shocked the public and which involved groups of men raping and trafficking vulnerable young girls. There were arrests or prosecutions of men in 11 towns and cities including Derby, Oldham, Rochdale, Oxford and Peterborough. In some cases, the men had targeted residential children's homes to find vulnerable victims.

Typically, groups of men would befriend and groom girls at places like taxi ranks and fast food outlets and, after forming relationships with them, would go on to abuse them, in some cases trafficking them across the country and selling them to others. A "race"/culture element emerged, with the perpetrators in some cases being primarily of Asian, particularly Pakistani, heritage. Most of the young victims were white and many were from disadvantaged backgrounds, including some in the care system, living in children's homes. There were claims that staff were reluctant to intervene in some cases for fear of being classed as racist. (More broadly, we know that CSE perpetrators come from every ethnic background.)

Professor Alexis Jay (2014) estimated that at least 1,400 children were subjected to appalling sexual exploitation in Rotherham between 1997 and 2013, in her report into the events and the shameful shortcomings of the local authority and police response. It makes distressing reading but it shows how ruthless the perpetrators can be. Victims were raped by multiple perpetrators, abducted and trafficked to other cities in England. They were beaten, threatened with guns, doused in petrol and threatened with being *set* alight if they said they were going to tell what had happened to them.

Inappropriate relationships

This includes cases in which the perpetrator is much older than the victim and exerts an unhealthy control over him or her.

In an interview featured on the Barnardo's website, one girl, called Nadine, describes how she met a much older "boyfriend" when she was just 14. Nadine describes the conflict between her and her mother, and her mother's attempts to keep her safe by keeping her at home and taking away her phone. But Nadine was oblivious to the risks; she began running away from home to spend time with older men. She was impressed by their cars and money and flattered by the attention:

> I thought it was really good to have an older boyfriend with money and cars. For someone to treat you like you're somebody when you don't feel like you have been – it's the best feeling.

(Barnardo's, no date)

By the age of 15 she was having sex and believes that, if not for the support she eventually received from a Barnardo's worker, she would have ended up on drugs or having sex for money. The Barnardo's worker was able to get through to Nadine by spelling out the nature and signs of exploitative relationships, which Nadine then recognised as features of her own relationships with the older men.

Sexual abuse by adults in a position of trust

The imbalance of power between a child and an adult who is the child's teacher, church leader, youth group leader, sports coach or music teacher – or even a television celebrity – can make a child susceptible to grooming and sexual abuse. This does not usually fit the definition of child sexual exploitation (see pp 5–7) and therefore we have not covered it in detail in this book.

In fact, in some cases the victim's parents are also skilfully groomed by the abuser into believing that they are a trusted "friend of the family" or even a suitable "boyfriend" for their child.

> Many sexual offenders give gifts to the child's caregiver. They might offer to babysit, take the children on holidays or do some other unsupervised activities that do not include the primary caregiver. Some offenders deliberately target those living below the poverty line, where such offers can be even more difficult to turn down and can seem very helpful at the time.

(Smith, 2015)

As with other types of CSE, children may fear not being believed if they tell; they may fear getting into trouble or being blamed; they may feel guilty or that it is their fault. Abusers often convince their victims of all of these things.

Perpetrators are not exclusively male. Some cases involve women in a position of trust, such as teachers.

The party-lifestyle model

One relatively recent method is the "party" model, in which young people are invited to parties and offered drink and drugs. Young people are there with their friends and initially it can seem like they are being given a good time. But at some point they are told they are now expected to provide sexual favours in return. They can find it difficult to withdraw from the party scene.

Charlotte Nutland, Training Manager of Basis Training & Education, writes that over the past few years workers at the organisation's charitable project, Isis, have observed the emergence of this new model of grooming. In a guest blog on the Safeguarding Children E-Academy website, she explains that this model differs from other types of CSE as it involves grooming whole groups of young people.

Typically, young people are groomed by other young people and invited to parties across their locality. These parties are held at a range of venues: hotels, flats, bars and in the summer months we were even informed about "tent parties".

Young people are invited in numbers which gives friendship groups the feeling of security. However, this is an intentional ploy to ensure that the group of young people are all involved in the process and therefore view the situation as "normal". Moreover, it gives the perpetrators access to a greater number of young people.

The parties are often set up purely with the intention of grooming and exploiting young people. Drugs and alcohol are usually offered for free as an incentive to attend more parties – this technique engages groups of young people who see the parties as fun, harmless and enjoyable.

It is only after weeks of attending these parties that repayment is discussed. Sometimes, perpetrators use the fact that young people have "enjoyed" their offering of drugs and alcohol and suggest they need to find a way of paying back if they want to continue to attend more parties.

What makes Party Lifestyle particularly challenging is the number of perpetrators present at the parties who are often introduced under aliases or with nicknames. Moreover, usually when young people are asked to "repay" for their consumption of drink, drugs, takeaways, phone credit, etc, they often oblige as either they don't want to be left out of the parties and/or they're scared.

The transition from young people receiving tangible gifts to the common use of phone credit, takeaways, drugs and alcohol make it increasingly more difficult to identify certain signs of CSE.

(Nutland, no date)

Parties and powerful individuals with links to Northern Ireland paramilitary groups

In 2014, the report of a major Inquiry into CSE in Northern Ireland was published. The Inquiry followed investigations by police into the sexual exploitation of a number of young people aged 13 to 18. It revealed that some perpetrators had links to paramilitary groups and used their connection to those groups to engender fear. Most of the victims were in residential care but some were living with their own families.

Many of those consulted by the Inquiry expressed the opinion that Northern Ireland was not experiencing the type of organised exploitation seen in Rochdale or Rotherham.

Nevertheless, the Inquiry received accounts of organised gangs linked with trafficking and drug dealing. Trafficking into, out of, or within Northern Ireland, can be a form of CSE, and drug dealing is often associated with CSE. Northern Ireland does not have the type of street gang culture identified in reports by the Office of the Children's Commissioner for England, as being associated with some forms of CSE.

The particular Northern Ireland dimension reported to the Inquiry was the involvement of powerful individuals with purported links to paramilitary organisations. Reports about this came from individuals, organisations and professionals. No-one suggested that CSE was a targeted activity of paramilitary groups.

It was a case of individuals using the authority of their paramilitary links and the fear it engendered, to exploit children and young people. The Inquiry was told that there were bars dominated by members of paramilitary groups, where there were lock-ins after hours and sexual exploitation took place. It is important to state that no-one identified names or locations in relation to these events. Some told us that they feared for their lives if they were suspected of having done so.

The party house scenario featured highly in discussions with agencies and young people. It is difficult to estimate the extent to which these are occasions for CSE because young people do not consider themselves as victims, even when they can acknowledge the vulnerabilities of friends and peers.

Parties are sometimes attended by, or organised by, adults. These were described as being mostly individuals or groups, rather than organised gangs, who coalesce around vulnerable children. Alcohol and drugs render the young people vulnerable.

(Marshall, 2014)

Other types of CSE

There are other types of CSE that do not easily fit any of the most recognised models. Take this example in which CSE was instigated by the child's mother:

I was 12, maybe a wee bit older, and I remember...and my mummy run out of drink and she says to me, there was fellas in the house and she says to one of them to take me up the stairs and she got me to go with this man for a bottle of vodka for her.

(Beckett, 2011)

CSE in children and young people trafficked from abroad

This book does not aim to address the issue of CSE in children and young people trafficked from abroad as it is outside its scope. Some of the same features clearly apply: traffickers may groom the child (and in some cases the child's parents) into believing they can be trusted, and there is a huge sense of betrayal when the child realises later that they have been tricked. Most victims are trafficked for financial gain. They are controlled with violence, or threats of violence towards them and their families, kept isolated or locked up and used by people who want to profit from their exploitation. The risks to their safety, physical health, sexual and reproductive health and mental health are considerable.

Their care plan needs to – as far as possible – protect them and minimise any risk of traffickers being able to re-involve them in exploitative activities. Foster carers and residential workers need to be vigilant about anything unusual such as cars waiting outside their home and telephone enquiries about the child.

For more information, see *Safeguarding Children who may have been Trafficked: Practice guidance* (DfE and Home Office, 2011).

2 Which children are at risk and what do we know about the signs of CSE?

Risk factors and vulnerabilities

No child is immune to becoming a victim of CSE. There are many different routes by which a child or young person can be victimised, involving a complex interplay of factors. Some of these factors relate to the child or young person themselves, while others are structural, e.g. being in residential care or living in a neighbourhood in which gang activity is rife.

The Government guidance on CSE, published in 2017, lists the following vulnerabilities as examples of the types of things children can experience that might make them more susceptible to child sexual exploitation:

- having a prior experience of neglect, physical and/or sexual abuse;
- lack of a safe/stable home environment, now or in the past (domestic violence or parental substance misuse, mental health issues or criminality, for example);
- recent bereavement or loss;
- social isolation or social difficulties;
- absence of a safe environment to explore sexuality;
- economic vulnerability;
- homelessness or insecure accommodation status;
- connections with other children and young people who are being sexually exploited;
- family members or other connections involved in adult sex work;
- having a physical or learning disability;

- being in care (particularly those in residential care and those with interrupted care histories);

- sexual identity.

Not all children and young people with these vulnerabilities will experience child sexual exploitation. Child sexual exploitation can also occur without any of these vulnerabilities being present.

(DfE, 2017, p8)

In terms of CSE that takes place or is initiated online, experts consider that children who show vulnerabilities in the "real world" may also be more vulnerable online than their peers. However, it is also the case that children and young people who would not be perceived as typically vulnerable (in the ways outlined above) are also coming to harm as a result of online sexual bullying, grooming and exploitation.

A Barnardo's report (Barnardo's, 2011) found that younger children were increasingly at risk of sexual exploitation – the average age of users of its services had fallen to around 13 in 2011.

In a more recent Barnardo's survey (Fox and Kalkan, 2016), it was said that the demographic of the service users the charity supports has been changing due to the influence of the internet on CSE:

... in the past, our practitioners used to provide support to children who were vulnerable due to a lack of parental support. Now the internet has meant that children who have no existing vulnerabilities and do have parental protection can become victims.

(Fox and Kalkan, 2016)

There are some common preconceptions about CSE victims, e.g. that they are almost always young white women. However, the report of the Office of the Children's Commissioner's Inquiry into CSE in Gangs and Groups points out that, although victims are predominantly girls and young women:

- *children and young people from a range of ages, both girls and young women and boys and young men, of a range of ethnicities, who identify as heterosexual, homosexual, lesbian or bisexual, and some who are disabled, have been sexually exploited in either gangs or groups.*

- *Furthermore, children from loving and secure homes can be abused in gangs and groups, as well as children with pre-existing vulnerabilities.*

  (Berelowitz *et al*, 2012, p82)

A review of the evidence (Brown *et al*, 2016) on risk indicators and protective factors for both child sexual abuse and exploitation was carried out by Coventry University on behalf of the Early Intervention Foundation.

It found that there is a lack of good quality research on the risk and protective factors for becoming either a victim or a perpetrator of child sexual abuse or CSE. In fact, the only two strongly evidenced indicators for becoming a victim were:

- being disabled;
- being in residential care.

The report points out that researchers who have spoken to victims or looked at risk factors have also identified the following common variables, though the evidence for these is less strong:

- alcohol and/or drug abuse (though it is unclear whether this precedes or results from the abuse or exploitation);
- going missing, running away and escaping from abuse and other difficulties within the family (running away can result in the child being homeless, leading to vulnerabilities that can increase the risk of CSE; equally, it can be a sign that CSE is happening);
- being involved in gangs and groups.

  (Brown *et al*, 2016)

Children living in residential children's homes

Residential care homes have improved their awareness of CSE and their protection of children at risk since the Parliamentary Inquiry in 2012 into Children who go Missing from Care (All Party Parliamentary Group (APPG) for Runaway and Missing Children and Adults and the APPG for Looked after Children and Care Leavers, 2012) (see 'Providing support in children's homes', page 86).

The 2012 Inquiry heard that perpetrators target children's homes specifically because of the high vulnerability of the children there and how easily they could make contact with them. The Office of the Children's Commissioner for England submitted evidence that it had:

> ...been informed about children's homes being targeted by perpetrators of child sexual exploitation, with multiple children across extended periods of time being groomed and abused by the same perpetrators

Sue Berelowitz, Deputy Children's Commissioner for England, told the Inquiry that:

> These children are particularly vulnerable because they often feel unloved, and frankly they are often unloved, so they are very susceptible to being groomed by men who tell them how much they love them, and give them gifts. It is easy to see how such children can fall into the grip of exploiters... The young person can be left feeling deeply conflicted – wanting to escape and yet being drawn to their exploiter. When a young person feels unloved they are vulnerable to someone who says 'I love you so much I want to share you with all my friends'.

(Oral evidence session to the APPG Inquiry into Children Missing from Care)

An unnamed former care worker in Rotherham has told how sex abusers picked up girls as young as 11 from their children's home and in some cases sent taxis to collect them, making no attempt to disguise what they were doing:

> The taxi drivers would get to know the girls while working on official council business... The girls would be taken by cab from the home to schools. But they would quickly start grooming them, giving them drugs and alcohol...

> Young girls told the Inquiry they actively avoided using taxis at night. Drivers would take the longest route possible and ask them how old they were. The conversations would become flirtatious, often with references to sex.

> Girls told how they would sometimes exchange sexual favours for lifts in taxis.

(Perry, 2014)

Gender

Many boys are also victims of CSE, though this is not always so readily recognised by professionals. Just like girls, boys can be intimidated by the use of violence, or threats of violence.

In an interview featured on the Barnardo's website, a young man named Samuel describes how his sexual exploitation began. At the age of 14, a friend introduced Samuel to a man he had met via the internet, and the man subsequently introduced Samuel to other men. Samuel was impressed by their money, and initially the relationships made him feel grown up.

But things turned sour and Samuel was being physically hurt. When he tried to distance himself, he was beaten up in the street.

> I got a phone call a couple of days later, saying 'Don't try to get away from me or it will happen again'.

(Barnardo's, no date)

Samuel's intimidation was complete; his exploiters knew where he lived, where he went to school and who his friends were. Fortunately he was eventually helped to escape from the situation by a Barnardo's CSE service.

Boys and young males may be sexually exploited by older men who make contact with them on the streets, in pubs, parks and other places and online. Young men – either gay or straight – may be drawn into having sex with older men, for money or other reasons. And there are also cases in which boys are seduced by older women in a position of trust, such as teachers.

There is little support on offer for the victims, who can in any case be reluctant to seek out services related to sexual abuse. Some victims go on to become perpetrators.

Young male victims often present differently from female victims. The signs and symptoms of their CSE often point to youth offending rather than CSE. Just like girls and young women, they may be involved in other crimes, either being coerced into it by their exploiters, as a reaction to the CSE (e.g. damaging a perpetrator's car) or as a "survival" crime, such as stealing food or money because they are penniless and on the street. Boys' behaviour is often interpreted and treated differently.

Just like female CSE victims, some boys might not recognise themselves as victims or they may be unwilling or afraid to tell anyone. Also, professionals are often less likely to ask boys the right questions or to spot the signs. Some boys might even prefer to be perceived as an offender rather than as someone who is being sexually exploited because of the stigma associated with the latter.

Greg (not his real name) was a victim of CSE that went unrecognised by many of the professionals with whom he came into contact. He believes they misinterpreted his difficulties because of his gender.

Greg came out as gay at the age of 12 and all his school friends ostracised him. His relationship with his single parent father broke down. He was depressed and isolated but no-one – including his social worker – offered any help.

He met a man through a gay social networking site who had claimed to be 18 but was actually 26, though by this point Greg was so desperate for a friend that he didn't care. The man and his friends introduced 12-year-old Greg to drink and drugs and bought him a mobile phone, clothes and trainers. At times they also physically hurt him. Greg's social worker interpreted his injuries, unexplained money and new clothes as signs that he was in a gang and referred him to a targeted prevention project for young people in gangs.

Greg was taken into foster care six months later but his (still unrecognised) sexual exploitation became even more extreme – he was being sent around the UK to meet groups of men who were so violent towards him that he twice ended up in the hospital accident and emergency unit. But he was too afraid to make a statement to the police. Eventually, at 13, he told a youth offending worker what was going on and social services were informed – but even after this, he says, nothing was done to help him.

On one occasion, one of his exploiters punched him in the face in the middle of a busy town centre but no-one stepped in – because, he believes, he was male and "boys fight" – even though his attacker was 13 years older.

Finally, after 18 months of horrific sexual exploitation, Greg's substance misuse and mental health reached such a dangerous point that he was admitted to a psychiatric hospital and was then at last referred to a Barnardo's CSE service.

He says that, all along, professionals had been making assumptions about his behaviour based on the fact that he was male and that if a girl had exhibited the same behaviours and signs of abuse, the CSE would have been recognised and measures would have been taken to safeguard her.

We must end the gender stereotyping that blocks these boys and young men from being safeguarded. Believe me, their abusers are relying on it.

(The Blast Project, www.mesmac.co.uk/projects/blast/for-boys-and-young-men/real-life-stories)

Probably because there are more CSE services aimed at girls, girls are referred more, and tend to disclose more often than boys. If you take a proactive approach and look for boy victims you will find them, says Phil Mitchell, Project Co-ordinator of The Blast Project, the UK's leading male-only CSE service.

In 2015, The Blast Project completed the national male CSE development project "Excellence for Boys". This project was funded by the Department for Education and saw The Blast Project work in collaboration with CSE services in 20 local authorities; resulting in the number of boys identified as being at risk of CSE increasing from 91 to 249.

(The Blast Project, 2016)

The Blast Project has found that, in educational sessions on CSE, boys tend to say they believe they have to deal with things on their own, whereas girls tend to say they would tell people.

There is variation in how police forces respond to possible CSE, he says. While some police forces are excellent, in others:

If a boy is found having travelled miles from home he will just be put on a train or a bus and sent home, whereas a girl would be referred to a CSE service. And the police don't respond to parents' concerns about boys in the same way they do about girls.

(Phil Mitchell, Project Co-ordinator, The Blast Project, speaking at *Tackling Child Sexual Exploitation: Prevention and Protection, Children & Young People Now* conference, December 2016.)

In the context of street gangs, there is sexual violence towards and exploitation of young men as well as young women. Former gang member Gwenton Sloley, who now runs a project to rehabilitate former gang members, has spoken about the use of sexual violence towards males.

The sexual abuse that happens in gangs has a power element. What we have found is some gang members will use sexual abuse as a tool to degrade a person, film it and then put it on social media as blackmail or to say, 'I'm so dangerous; I raped him'. It is used now as a weapon and it's increased a lot because it goes viral within seconds.

(Quoted in Vyas, 2015)

Interconnected conditions for CSE

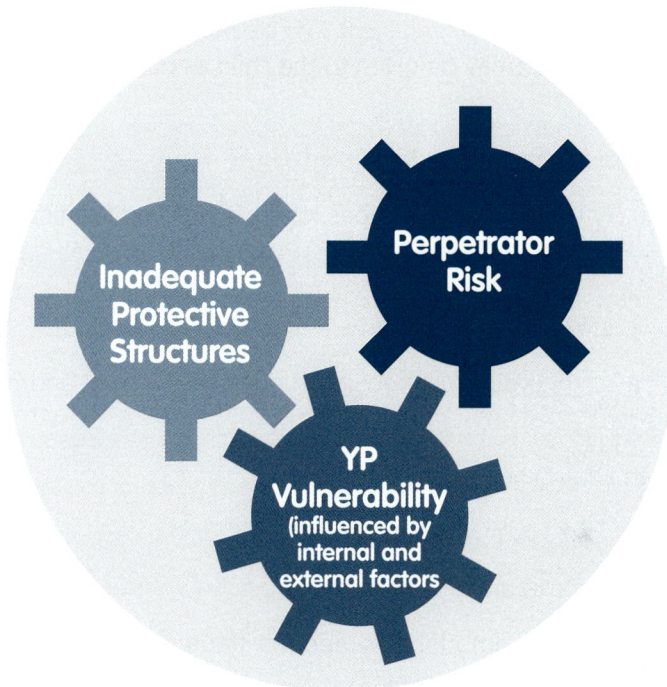

(Beckett, 2011)

Various factors interact with each other to culminate in an individual child becoming sexually exploited. These include the child's own vulnerabilities; exposure to someone who would take advantage of them; the opportunities for perpetrators to come into contact with children, which have expanded due to social networking; and inadequate protective structures around the child.

Possible warning signs

Some of the following are warning signs that a child may be or is being sexually exploited, according to the report by the Office of the Children's Commissioner:

- going missing from home or care;
- physical injuries;
- drug or alcohol misuse (may be given to the child as part of the grooming process);
- involvement in offending;
- repeated sexually transmitted infections, pregnancies and termination;
- absence from school;
- change in physical appearance;
- evidence of sexual bullying/vulnerability through the internet and/or social networking sites;
- being estranged from their family;
- receipt of gifts from unknown sources;
- recruiting others into exploitative situations;
- poor mental health (e.g. emotional symptoms, trauma symptoms, problem behaviours, problems in relationships);
- self-harm or thoughts of or attempts at suicide.

(Berelowitz, 2012, p114)

Clearly, none of these signs on their own can be taken as indicating that a child or young person is a victim of CSE. It's also likely that there are other indicators that have not yet been identified. And relying on signs like these could mean missing some children and young people who are not behaving in these ways but who are still being sexually exploited.

There is an overlap between the indicators that CSE may be occurring and the factors that make children and young people more vulnerable to CSE.

...There is some overlap between what constitutes a "vulnerability factor" (something that may enhance vulnerability to child sexual exploitation) and

a "risk indicator" (something that may indicate harm is occurring). Substance misuse is a good example. Drug use may increase a child/young person's vulnerability to exploitation because it provides an abuser with a potential route for access and control; and victims of sexual exploitation may turn to substance misuse to cope with what they have experienced. If we are to pitch our responses appropriately, it is important we understand the nature of the relationship between the indicator/vulnerability and the risk/harm (which is contributing to the other?).

(Beckett *et al*, 2017)

Assessing the "risk" of CSE: some concerns about checklists and toolkits

Young victims rarely come forward to disclose that they are experiencing sexual exploitation and the reasons for this are complex (see Chapter 5). If there are suspicions that a young person is being sexually exploited, they are likely to be referred to a practitioner who has to try to work out what is going on in their life and their sexual relationships.

For the last decade, practitioners have been using CSE "toolkits" or "checklists of risk factors or signs of sexual exploitation" as a diagnostic measure of whether the child they are working with is at low, medium or high risk of CSE. For example, the indicators include things like "child has unaccounted-for money or goods including mobile phones, drugs and alcohol, always has credit on phone without access to money"; "stays out overnight without explanation"; and "adults/older youths loitering outside the child's usual place of residence or school".

However, some workers have serious concerns about these toolkits and point out that they have not been rigorously tested and there is no evidence base for their effectiveness or reliability (most of the studies on CSE victims have not compared victims with non-victim groups, therefore there was no control group). They feel there is an over-reliance on risk indicator lists.

As the systems have become more sophisticated and as teams have started to work together to tackle child sexual exploitation, risk indicator lists that were once used to loosely guide professionals turned into mandatory, rigid, diagnostic scoring systems within which indicators were labelled "low", "medium" or "high" risk of CSE occurring without any study taking place to look at whether that labelling was accurate. Not only were indicators resigned to this labelling but children, too, were beginning to be labelled as "low", "medium" or "high" risk of CSE depending on how many of the relevant indicators were ticked off on the checklist.

(Eaton, 2016)

Another issue is that some of the supposed "at risk" indicators clearly show that the child is already a victim who is actively being harmed, as opposed to "at high risk", e.g. "signs of physical or sexual injuries with no explanation" and "being seen in hotspots, i.e. known houses, recruiting grounds or parties, 'crack houses'."

A child classed as "medium risk" in one authority could be classed as "high risk" in another, so they could be allocated a different service and level of expertise.

Indicators of CSE can be somewhat stereotypical, which means that professionals could be completely missing certain groups of victims because these groups do not display the usual indicators. Most checklists have been designed with girls in mind rather than boys, and consequently CSE in boys may be missed or misinterpreted if practitioners rely too much on these. In boys, the signs of CSE might be similar to the signs of involvement in offending (see above, p28).

The researchers said:

There is a lack of strong research evidence on which to base risk assessment tools. In order to develop these tools practitioners have had to rely on a range of sources of information including case reviews, local authority reviews, practice experience and/or the few emerging, mainly qualitative, exploratory studies recently published on CSE. This raises concerns about the quality of the evidence on which they are based. In addition, not surprisingly, given the high profile of investigations into large scale gang-related CSE in a number of local authorities, it could be argued that the tools may have been developed with this particular type of CSE in mind and thus possibly other types of CSE, and/or newly emerging forms of CSE, could be missing from these assessment tools.

(Eaton, 2016)

The researchers stress that professionals should be allowed and encouraged to use their professional judgement and that they should use tools and checklists only to underpin decision-making rather than determine decisions.

3 CSE: recognition and response from agencies

How do cases come to light?

CSE is an unusual crime in that victims rarely report it to the police. Indeed, they rarely disclose it to anyone (see Chapter 5 for the reasons for this).

Most victims come to attention because someone has noticed the signs or symptoms. In many cases, worried parents or teachers realise that something is very wrong with a child and will ask them about it or seek help, for example, from children's social care services or another organisation.

The child may be taking out their feelings on others (externalising) by becoming aggressive and violent, becoming angry and hostile towards their parents and others, and even becoming sexually aggressive towards others. (Sometimes, of course, the child's own behaviour is seen as the problem, and adults don't realise that CSE is the cause.) He or she may misuse substances as a way of self-medicating or escaping the feelings; in some cases, victims self-harm or show their mental anguish in other ways, including suicide attempts. Some develop serious psychiatric disorders. Parents or other adults may get in touch with the police or social care on the basis of seeing worrying signs, such as the child staying out late with no explanation, or going missing.

In some cases, concerns about a child are picked up by a school nurse or when he or she attends a health setting such as an accident and emergency service, minor injury unit or sexual health service. Health professionals may need to treat the child for physical or sexual assault, a sexually transmitted infection or unwanted pregnancy, or drug, alcohol or substance misuse, self-harm or even a suicide attempt.

Sometimes children are found by the police in situations where they are being or have been sexually exploited, either when the police have been alerted to suspicions about CSE, or to the fact that the child has gone missing, or by chance. For example, they might be found on the street, or in a building that's been raided by the police. There may have been a trigger incident for police involvement; members of the public may report concerns about incidents or particular locations. The child or young person may have gone missing from their home or children's home and been found somewhere away from home – sometimes a long way from home.

What happens next?

If the child is picked up by the police having been missing, found in a distressed state or under the influence of alcohol or drugs, and there are suspicions of CSE, they will contact the local authority children's services. Police can use their powers to remove the child to a safe place. If this has happened, or if someone has contacted children's services with concerns, the next steps are likely to be the following:

- An assessment to establish whether the child requires immediate protection and urgent action; or, the child is in need and should be assessed under section 17 of the Children Act 1989 (England and Wales) or section 22 of the Children (Scotland) Act 1995, or section 18 of the Children (Northern Ireland) Order 1995; or, there is reasonable cause to suspect that the child is suffering, or likely to suffer, significant harm, and whether enquiries must be made and the child assessed under section 47 of the Children Act (England and Wales), or section 22 of the Children (Scotland) Act 1995, or section 18 of the Children (Northern Ireland) Order 1995.

- If there is a risk to the life of a child or a likelihood of serious immediate harm, local authority social workers, the police or NSPCC must use their statutory child protection powers to act immediately to secure the safety of the child.

- If the child is identified as being in need, a social worker should lead a multi-agency assessment under section 17. Where this leads the social worker to suspect that the child is suffering or likely to suffer significant harm, the local authority should hold a strategy discussion to enable it to decide, with other agencies, whether to initiate enquiries under section 47.

The police will lead investigations into possible criminal offences (see later in this chapter), while the local authority has the lead for the section 47 enquiries and assessment of the child's welfare.

If the child is considered to be at risk of harm, this will be followed by a child protection conference, which may decide that the child needs to be the subject of a Child Protection Plan. If so, a plan will be developed by the child's key worker together with other members of a core group, who will provide or commission the interventions that the child and family need.

The social worker's risk assessment needs to take into account the child's age and, as far as they can ascertain, any other power imbalance, overt aggression and/or acts of coercion or bribery; misuse of substances that the abuser may have supplied in order to disinhibit the child or young person; whether the sexual partner(s) is known to agencies and/or the police; and whether the child is being groomed or is otherwise unable to make an informed choice about engaging in sexual activity.

If a child or young person was found after going missing, they must be offered a "safe and well" check by the police and a "return home interview" by someone independent of the police, to try to ascertain what has happened. All local authorities must have a Runaway and Missing from Home and Care Joint Protocol that sets out the roles and responsibilities of various multi-agency partners (including children's services and the police) when a child goes missing from home or care. Suspected or known cases of CSE will be referred to the local multi-agency CSE team, hub or panel.

Multi-agency CSE teams

Many local authorities have set up multi-agency safeguarding hubs (MASH) or teams to co-ordinate their response to sexual abuse and exploitation, and a number of these have dedicated CSE teams. A multi-agency environment is crucial to getting a child the right service at the right time for them.

There are likely to be representatives from the police, children's services, health services, CAMHS (child and adolescent mental health services), youth offending teams, education, and voluntary sector organisations working with young people on drugs and alcohol abuse, sexual health and/or CSE. Ideally the team will also have a specialist parents' support worker.

The professionals discuss specific children and young people who have come to their attention, what the concerns are about them, what support they need and what actions are needed to keep them safe. They also share intelligence, e.g. about any links between the victims, CSE local "hotspots" and possible offenders, which helps the police investigate offences and helps other agencies to understand the nature of what is happening to the children and young people they are working with.

The value of different agencies working together is that they can find out what is happening locally, see the bigger picture and get a better understanding of the context in which CSE is taking place. Sharing information can result in people realising there are links between cases, which may help the police to identify the perpetrators.

The role of the Local Safeguarding Children Board

Local Safeguarding Children Boards are partnerships established by the 2004 Children Act in England and Wales. The LSCB brings together the local authority, police, probation service, youth offending team, health service and other agencies, which are expected to work closely with organisations from voluntary and community services to set policies that safeguard the welfare of children and young people. Every local authority area must have one by law.

In Scotland, Child Protection Committees (CPCs) were first established in each local authority area in 1991. These were strengthened in 2005 and today there are 31 CPCs, consisting of representation from police, health services, local authorities, children's services, and community planning structures and relevant voluntary sector forums, amongst others. In Northern Ireland, the Safeguarding Board for Northern Ireland was established following the passing of the Safeguarding Board Act (Northern Ireland) 2011. The SBNI is required to establish five independently chaired Safeguarding Panels.

The identification of a child or young person involved in sexual exploitation, or at risk of being drawn into sexual exploitation, should always trigger the agreed local safeguarding children procedures to ensure the child's safety and welfare, and to enable the police to gather criminal evidence about the perpetrators. See the Appendix for a more detailed outline of the LSCBs' role and responsibilities.

The National Working Group and National CSE Response Unit

The NWG (formerly The National Working Group for Sexually Exploited Children and Young People) is a charitable organisation formed as a UK network of over 12,000 CSE practitioners who disseminate information to other professionals working on the issue of CSE and trafficking within the UK.

In March 2015, the Government published a report into dealing with CSE, which included plans to develop a national taskforce to assist practitioners to tackle this form of child abuse. The Government provided the NWG with £1.24 million to develop the taskforce and deliver its objectives. In 2016, the NWG launched a team of specialists to help support professionals tackling CSE, which has been named the National CSE Response Unit.

The CSE Response Unit team comprises of specialists in safeguarding, police and justice, health, education and community engagement, youth participation and parental support. It is responsible for:

- providing support and guidance to practitioners at an operational level;

- assisting local authorities, police forces, local safeguarding boards and other organisations with strategic planning and responses to CSE;

- supporting professionals via a resources library, containing a wide range of tools aimed at addressing CSE;

- operating an out-of-hours helpline for professionals who require immediate assistance;

- developing a register of skills and knowledge consisting of practitioners and agencies who can be deployed to assist professionals and agencies in tackling CSE;

- helping agencies to "operationalise" recommendations from reviews, inspections and operations.

The CSE Response Unit operates on a voluntary basis and works with professionals and agencies following a request for assistance – there is no mandatory requirement to work with the unit.

Professionals can call the response unit on 0300 303 3032.

The criminal justice process, working with the police and supporting the child through a court case

4

What does the law say about CSE?

Children – whatever age they are – should not be held responsible or blamed for what adults have done to them. The fact that a young person is 16 or 17 years old and has reached the legal age of being able to consent to sex should not be taken to mean that they are therefore consenting and no longer at risk of sexual exploitation. These young people are still legally defined as children and can still suffer significant harm as a result of sexual exploitation. Their right to support and protection from harm should not be ignored or de-prioritised by services because they are over 16.

There is no specific offence of child sexual exploitation. But the Sexual Offences Act 2003 (which applies to England and Wales) introduced a range of new criminal offences that recognised the grooming, coercion and control of children and young people under 18. The Act:

- says that children under 13 cannot legally consent to sex (it is statutory rape);
- says that sexual activity by adults with children under 16 is unlawful;
- provides further information regarding child sex offences committed by children or young people under 18;
- makes it an offence to arrange or facilitate commission of a child sex offence (child under 16);
- makes it an offence to pay for the sexual services of a child;
- makes it an offence to meet a child under 16 following sexual grooming;

- covers sexual offences of children under 18 where the offender has abused a position of trust;

- covers exploitation of children through prostitution and pornography for children up to age 18.

The law on sexual communication with a child

To tackle the early stages of grooming, a new offence of *sexual communication with a child* came into effect in April 2017. It covers both online and offline communication, including through social media, email and letters. Adult groomers will face up to two years in prison and automatically be placed on the sex offenders register.

Internal trafficking

Internal sex trafficking of adults or children is a crime under section 58 of the Sexual Offences Act. This makes it an offence to arrange, or facilitate, the movement of someone within the UK for the purpose of sexual exploitation. There is no minimum movement requirement, so movements within a city or even a single street qualify.

Indecent photos

Section 1 of the Protection of Children Act 1978 (England and Wales) makes it an offence to take, make, distribute or show indecent photos or pseudo-photos of children. Similar legislation exists in Scotland – Section 52, Civic Government (Scotland) Act 1982 – as well as in Northern Ireland – section 3, Protection of Children (Northern Ireland) Order 1978. Section 160 of the Criminal Justice Act 1988 makes it an offence to possess indecent photos or pseudo-photos of children. Section 84 of the Criminal Justice and Public Order Act 1994, titled *Obscene Publications and Indecent Photographs of Children*, applies all over the UK. The Sexual Offences Act 2003 extended the meaning of "child" for the purposes of these two provisions to children aged under 18 (rather than 16); so did the Protection of Children and Prevention of Sexual Offences (Scotland) Act 2005 and in Northern Ireland, the Sexual Offences (Northern Ireland) Order 2008.

Other sexual offences

The police and Crown Prosecution Service often try to convict using other sexual offences, such as rape or false imprisonment, or use other legislation to disrupt the activity of abusers, such as the Abduction Act 1984. So not all cases are recorded as child sexual exploitation. Scotland and Northern Ireland have their own laws – for more information see www.fpa.org.uk/factsheets/law-on-sex.

The age of consent for sex

Throughout the UK, the age of consent to any form of sexual activity is 16 for both men and women, though the law protects people from sexual exploitation up to the age of 18. It is an offence for anyone to have any sexual activity with a person under the age of 16. However, it is recognised that some under-16s will have a mutually consenting sexual relationship and the law will not prosecute unless it involves abuse or exploitation. The law also gives extra protection to young people who are 16 to 17 years old and it is illegal:

- to take, show or distribute indecent photographs of them

- to pay for or arrange for their sexual services

- for a person in a position of trust (for example, teachers, care workers) to engage in sexual activity with anyone under 18 in relation to whom he/she is in a position of trust.

If a person engages in sexual activity with a child aged 12 or below, they may not use the defence that they believed the child was over 16 and that they believed they were engaging in lawful sexual activity; children of this age are deemed legally incapable of giving their consent to any form of sexual activity. An offence can result in a maximum sentence of life imprisonment for rape, sexual assault by penetration, and causing or inciting a child to engage in sexual activity.

The law on grooming

England and Wales

It is an offence to befriend a child on the internet or by other online means and meet or intend to meet the child with the intention of abusing them. A Risk of Sexual Harm Order, introduced by the Sexual Offences Act, can be imposed on adults in order to prevent them from engaging in inappropriate sexual behaviour such as having sexual conversations with children online. The police can apply for such orders if they believe that someone poses a risk to young people under 16.

Northern Ireland

Sexual grooming is covered under the Sexual Offences (Northern Ireland) Order 2008. It is an offence for a person aged 18 or over to meet or communicate with a person aged under 16 two or more times and then subsequently meet or intend to meet them with the intention of committing a sexual offence.

Scotland

The offence of "grooming" was introduced under the Protection of Children and Prevention of Sexual Offences Act 2005. Grooming is described as a person intentionally developing a relationship with a young person under the age of 16 'in order to gain their trust and persuade them into vulnerable situations where they can then be sexually assaulted'. A Risk of Sexual Harm Order can be imposed on a person by the courts if that person's behaviour suggests they pose a risk of sexual harm to a particular child or to children generally.

(Reproduced from *The Law on Sex*, FPA website: www.fpa.org.uk)

Treating children and young people as victims, not criminals

Quite often the way young people involved in CSE are found is that they are picked up by the police when they are caught offending. They may have been forced to engage in criminality by their abusers or be doing it to get something they desperately need.

The Crown Prosecution Service is required to treat a child or young person who has been forced into prostitution or coerced into committing crimes as an abused child and a victim who needs help rather than as a defendant.

As part of the strategy discussion about CSE cases, the police must discuss the basis for any criminal investigation (of perpetrators) and any relevant processes that other agencies might need to know about, including the timing and methods of evidence gathering. The police will lead the criminal investigation where joint enquiries take place.

The "Achieving Best Evidence" interview

When CSE is suspected, the police will start to investigate. They will carry out an initial brief interview with the victim when the CSE is first reported or suspected and this will be followed at some point by a formal interview called an "Achieving Best Evidence" (ABE) interview.

"Making Justice Work" was a one-year research project at the University of Bedfordshire's International Centre: Researching Child Sexual Exploitation, Violence and Trafficking. Researchers Dr Helen Beckett and Dr Camille Warrington explored young people's experience of the criminal justice system in CSE cases and the way these could be improved. The research involved in-depth participatory research with young people and professionals and found much room for improvement at every stage of a young person's journey through the criminal justice process, including the ABE interview.

ABE interviews are video recorded interviews designed to support vulnerable and intimidated victims and witnesses to provide reliable and accurate accounts of their victimisation, in keeping with their best interests and in a way which is fair. They serve a dual purpose; initially being utilised as an investigative tool and subsequently being shown as evidence in chief within court. Many young people did not, however, fully understand the significance of this dual purpose during the initial video recording.

(Beckett and Warrington, 2015)

The young people in the research, for the most part, felt intensely embarrassed about having to describe their experiences. Some of them found the style of questioning adopted by police intimidating or accusatory; they felt unprepared for, and unnerved by, the change of tone in questioning adopted by police once the formal ABE interview started. However, one young person described how the professionals involved in her case had supported her by taking time to build rapport, facilitate her sense of control, and fully explain the approach that the interviewers would adopt:

I think a good thing was that in my case they did prepare me. Like they came and picked me and my mam up, and although my mam had to stay outside while I was being interviewed I knew that she was there. They told me I could have a break whenever I wanted one and they kind of gave me a pre-warning – that when he [the police interviewer] goes in there he will have no emotion, and he'll be blank and just ask questions...He kind of warned me about that which was a good thing.

(Young person quoted in Beckett and Warrington, 2015)

The Crown Prosecution Service gives this guidance:

> A victim of child sexual abuse may not give their best and fullest account during their first recorded ["Achieving Best Evidence"] interview or statement. This may be for a variety of reasons: they could have been threatened; they might be fearful for themselves or their family; the offending may have been reported by others and they may be reluctant to co-operate at that stage. They might not have identified themselves as a victim or they could be fearful that the police will not believe their allegations. They may initially distrust the police and could well use the interview to test the credibility of the police.
>
> The account given may take a number of interviews, with the child or young person giving their account piecemeal, sometimes saving the "worst" till last, having satisfied themselves that they can trust the person to whom they are giving their account.
>
> Carefully thought out patient intervention by the police and other agencies can ultimately disrupt and break the link to the offender(s). A seemingly contradictory initial account is therefore not a reason in itself to disbelieve subsequent accounts given by the victim and these contradictory accounts should instead be seen as at least potentially symptomatic of the abuse.
>
> (Crown Prosecution Service, 2013)

Gathering evidence

The police will gather evidence and intelligence, to corroborate the child's account and see how the details of people and places may fit in with other cases they know about.

Social services, children's services, voluntary sector and other local support services and, if appropriate, parents or carers, should involve the police as early as possible to ensure that information critical to a prosecution case is not lost. Information can be gathered and collated even where the child or young person has not made a formal complaint.

In many cases, it takes a long time for a child or young person to recognise the exploitative nature of their relationship with the offender. Evidence needs to be gathered from very early on because otherwise crucial information could be lost or destroyed by the time the child is willing to tell.

When the child is living at home, parents and carers may be asked to help by gathering evidence that will be useful in constructing a case against the perpetrator(s). They can take an active role in information gathering, noting what they see and overhear and feeding this back to the right person. This might be, for example, time of phone calls, names mentioned by their child, Facebook comments and so on.

Other types of evidence that should be gathered to help build a case before the child or young person gives a statement include: obtaining DNA evidence, for example, from clothing the young person was wearing when they were with their abuser; descriptions of suspects; mobile phone evidence; CCTV footage; car number plates; house searches; and surveillance. Neighbours could be a useful source of other information about the wider context. Other useful information can sometimes be gathered from friends of the victims and their peer group, especially about the wider context.

In some areas the multi-agency CSE team includes an independent parent support worker (IPSW) whose role is to work with the parents of CSE victims to provide emotional and practical support. A parents' support worker advocates for parents and liaises between the parents and the police investigating the case and other statutory agencies. This person can ensure that any information is passed on to others in the multi-agency team, whose members may well be able to spot links between places and people mentioned by others.

The information that the IPSW provided each week was often substantial enough to generate new referrals for the team about other vulnerable young people. Some IPSWs have developed a system of logging concerns, which have proved to be especially useful for foster carers and residential care workers. "Provenance logs" capture relevant information for the police. IPSWs can train residential and foster care staff on how to record in these logs and include evidence in a section called 'How do you know it is true?'.

There is a distinction between information and intelligence and some frustrations can arise from parents when they share information that they think is intelligence and will be acted on. Some parents will have had negative experiences of phoning the police or social services to try and share information in the past. One of the important roles of the IPSW is to help parents understand the difference and act as a vessel to pass information on. The information may not be enough to act on; however, feeding it back to the CSE teams via an IPSW gives the police and partners the chance to formalise this information and turn some of it into intelligence that informs a bigger picture. In some cases, this process has culminated in a sophisticated network mapping that has led to a police operation targeting multiple offenders.

(PACE UK, 2014)

Children and young people interviewed for the Making Justice Work research talked about having to provide a range of personal items to the police for evidence, including personal mobile phones, laptops, items of clothing, photos and diaries. They felt disempowered and even punished by having their things taken away and not knowing if or when they would get them back. There were practical issues around having to continue to pay for a mobile phone contract while you were without your phone. But more than that, mobile phones play a central role in young people's friendships and support networks. Having them removed exacerbated their sense of isolation and/or physical insecurity, as one young person explained:

When they took my phone and that kind of took my safety away – because then...if anything was to happen between me going from home to school – I had no way of contacting anybody.

(Young person quoted in Beckett and Warrington, 2015)

Some young people did receive a replacement phone, but approaches to this seemed to be inconsistent. Professionals didn't recognise just how important phones were to the young people.

Will the child have to go to court?

It is the Crown Prosecution Service, not the police, that decides whether or not to prosecute the offender. This decision will depend on whether the CPS thinks there is sufficient evidence to provide a realistic prospect of conviction and a prosecution is required in the public interest. You can read the CPS's guidelines on prosecuting cases of child sexual abuse at the CPS website: http://www.cps.gov.uk/legal/a_to_c/child_sexual_abuse/.

In some cases, the child and/or the child's parents decide that they don't want the child to go through the ordeal of appearing in court as a witness, or the child may refuse to incriminate the perpetrator.

Children and young people often feel that they lose all control of what happens once they have reported the sexual exploitation, or it has come to the attention of the police.

> Several of the experts by experience [i.e. young victims] also reported losing control in relation to their choice as to whether or not to engage in criminal proceedings. Three expressed feeling pressured to engage with an investigation through guilt or fear – rather than choice – and being unaware about their rights in relation to this.

(Beckett and Warrington, 2015)

The police may still be able to disrupt the activities of the perpetrators in other ways, even if there is no prospect of being able to bring them to court. It may sometimes be possible to prosecute an offender even if a child or young person is unwilling to give evidence. For example, the police can now use forensic evidence, perhaps acquired from the child's clothes. If a child or young person is going to testify against their abuser, they will be given support along the way, and special measures are taken in court to protect young witnesses, including the possibility of being cross-examined in a "virtual" hearing rather than in the courtroom (see Chapter 6).

What else the police and local authority can do

As well as attempting to bring the perpetrators to justice for their CSE, the police often work in a number of other ways to disrupt the activities of the perpetrators. For example, they may work with the local authority to get better lighting installed, cut back foliage and install CCTV in known "hotspots". This lets the perpetrators know that the police are aware of what's going on. Licensing laws can be used to obtain information about people staying in hotels and guesthouses or to close down premises associated with child sexual exploitation.

They can obtain orders (see below) on an identified individual, investigate other types of crime, such as drugs or theft, increase police attention on individuals (checking car tax, road worthiness of car, etc), and increase police presence in suspected hotspots (both on the ground and online).

Below are some of the orders available to the police apart from bringing prosecutions for the CSE offences.

Sexual Risk Orders and Sexual Harm Prevention Orders

These are civil orders introduced in the Antisocial Behaviour, Crime and Policing Act 2014, and came into force in 2015 and apply across the UK. These give the police powers where their intelligence indicates that there is a risk of future harm. They can prevent certain behaviour that is not wrong in itself but that may become so because of the intentions behind it. Sexual Harm Prevention Orders can be used to impose restrictions on an individual who has been convicted or cautioned of a sexual or violent offence. Sexual Risk Orders do not require an individual to have been convicted or cautioned and can be used where there isn't enough evidence.

Child Abduction Warning Notices

The police can use Child Abduction Warning Notices (CAWNs) as a way of disrupting contact between a vulnerable child and an adult where there are concerns that the child may be at risk of harm including inappropriate relationships, sexual exploitation or involvement in crime. They identify a child and confirm that the suspect has no permission to associate with, contact or approach them. They apply to young people under the age of 16 (or under 18 if in local authority care). Issuing a CAWN is often part of ongoing police investigations; they make it impossible for a potentially abusive adult to claim that they did not know that the person they were in contact with was a vulnerable child. This can be used as evidence in court if any later abuse or other crime takes place.

The National Referral Mechanism

The National Referral Mechanism (NRM) is a framework for identifying and safeguarding victims of human trafficking or modern slavery. It applies to victims of both domestic and international trafficking and can be used in cases when a child is moved from one city to another within the UK, for example. It is designed to facilitate relevant multi-agency involvement, ensuring that the victim receives safe accommodation, appropriate protection, support and advice. Referrals to the NRM contribute to building evidence about trafficking and modern slavery, allowing the police to build a national picture and informing policy and practice in this area.

The Government's latest guidance to CSE, set out in Annex B (DfE, 2017), gives a fuller picture of the range of disruption measures, civil powers and criminal offences which may be used by practitioners as part of a strategy to tackle child sexual exploitation.

Working with the police

Some children and young people will already be working with the police before entering foster care or residential children's homes. But others may disclose what has happened to them after going into the placement, after which the police will become involved.

A young person may be unwilling to engage with the police and prosecuting authorities even in the absence of any specific threats from the perpetrator. This may be because they are mistrustful of authority, don't think it will achieve anything, are afraid of the consequences, or out of a misplaced sense of loyalty to the person or people who exploited them. This can, of course, make prosecutions very difficult.

A report in 2016 (HMIP, HMIC, CQC, Ofsted, 2016), which looked at the response to CSE of various agencies, including the police, showed that in some areas, police had learnt lessons from multi-agency operations or previous high-profile cases. This was resulting in skilled approaches to engaging with and supporting victims of CSE regardless of whether or not prosecutions would proceed. For example:

> Northumbria Police's "victim strategy" ensures that the service and support from the police is the same whether there is a prosecution or not. The approach to victims is applied whether the victim is a child or an adult. The "victim strategy" means that a trusted individual is identified for the victim to speak with. A meeting of those who know the young person is held to discuss risks and identify the "trusted individual" who can talk to the victim about risk, support and welfare and whether they want to be involved in a prosecution. This may be a social worker who can then take the statement from the child/young person. Some young people do not want to be involved in an "achieving best evidence" interview and therefore the victim is asked about how they want to tell the police about what happened. They may not want to tell the whole story and careful consideration is given to creative ways of explaining what has happened. The approach is characterised by persistence, patience, help and support for the victim, capturing evidence where possible. The approach adopted by the police is that every piece of information is valuable and if it looks like someone may be at risk, the team will routinely go and speak with them. Victims are supported through the court process and beyond. Victims may not be prepared immediately to give information but by maintaining relationships and contact, examples were

seen where young people had provided information at a later stage that had resulted in a prosecution.

(HMIP, HMIC, CQC, Ofsted, 2016)

Children and young people can find it tough, however:

The process of criminal investigations following a disclosure often proved challenging to the children. Although they had disclosed to [children's home] staff, children could be reluctant to tell their story again to the police... When children disclosed to the police, they could be asked to repeat the same details numerous times, for example, first to the investigating officer, and then again to a video camera. Interviewees felt that police procedures needed to be improved in recognition of how traumatic and momentous this process was for the child... Children also complained about not feeling that they were updated enough about the progress of an investigation, or that new information they provided did not seem to be taken seriously by the police, as when, for example, they passed on information to the police about the whereabouts of a perpetrator who was being investigated.

(La Valle and Graham, 2016)

If the CPS does decide to go ahead, it can take months between the child disclosing that they have been sexually exploited and going to court. Many young victims would benefit from counselling and therapy during this period, but this is not always offered. (See Chapter 6 for information about pre-trial therapy for young people.)

The child or young person may be offered support from other people, such as a victim liaison police officer and an independent sexual violence adviser. It helps a lot if they are kept informed about the progress of the investigation, when and whether it will go to court, and what to expect next.

The nature of police investigations means that:

...an initial period of concentrated, and sometimes intrusive, contact with police was often abruptly followed by periods of little or no contact. Some of the experts by experience described struggling to manage the shift in pace and described a sense of "being kept in the dark" ...and associated feelings of anxiety and stress.

(Beckett and Warrington, 2015)

During this period there are a number of difficulties for young people to face. Other people, including their peers, can find out about their involvement (for example, when police visit the young people at home or school or they need time off school) and they can feel judged and stigmatised by them. Young people responded that it also disrupted their schooling and family life and some felt guilty about the impact on their family. They also felt very vulnerable and afraid of reprisals as a result of the suspect knowing they were working with the police, especially if suspects were not remanded in custody. During this time, some perpetrators, or their friends and associates, can issue threats to dissuade the child (and/or their family and other potential witnesses) from going to court to give evidence against them.

If you are looking after a child and this happens, take any and all threats seriously and report them to the child's social worker and the police. Some young people are given witness protection by the police.

If the case is dropped

If the Crown Prosecution Service decides not to take things further and the case is dropped, that can be very hard for the child to take. You will need to explain what this means (i.e. it does not mean the police don't believe them).

NFA (no further action) decisions made by the police or CPS were upsetting for the young people in the Making Justice Work research, many of whom felt that professionals did not fully appreciate the impact and gravity of such decisions. And the professionals noted how the outcomes of previous cases in which young people were involved could sometimes unfairly inform decisions about whether to prosecute.

> It can kind of come across as if they're just like – 'Oh you know, there's not enough evidence – not enough facts there' – and then you question, like, well what was the point of me going through that?...You go through all this and you've gone through like the devastation of having to relive what happened, through your interviews, for them to turn around and say 'Nah – we're not going to take it any further'. Devastating – it is devastating.

(Young person quoted in Beckett and Warrington, 2015)

Waiting for the court case and going to court

As a parent or carer, you may need to support a child or young person who has to go to court to give evidence against the perpetrator. You and the child should get help and advice on this from the witness support or police liaison officer or other support worker. PACE UK offers a lot of good advice, including in a booklet called *Supporting Your Child in Court*.

A number of measures and recommendations have been introduced in recent years to improve the court process for young and vulnerable witnesses, to make it less intimidating, and to offer them more support and protection. For example, child sexual exploitation cases should be prosecuted by an advocate who understands CSE in front of judges and magistrates who are trained to understand CSE.

New measures that will spare rape victims the trauma of attending court are set to be rolled out across the country, starting in September 2017. Victims of rape and other sex crimes will have their cross-examination evidence pre-recorded and played during the trial rather than having to stand up in court with their attacker present.

Work to roll out pre-recorded evidence given by child victims of sexual offences has already begun, following a successful pilot scheme that showed child victims felt less pressure giving pre-trial evidence and were better able to recall events. It led to more guilty pleas and victims reporting a more positive experience of the court process. In an increasing number of cases, children and young people can give their evidence in private, or from a video link in a room outside the courtroom. This will suit some young people, while others would prefer to be in the courtroom giving evidence from behind a screen. They are supposed to be given this choice, though in practice this is not always explained to them.

Whether the child is going to give evidence in court or away from the courtroom, by video, it will be helpful for them if you can explain the process in terms they can understand – for instance, the roles of the judge, the jury, the prosecution and defence barristers and the aim of cross-examination. Explain to the child that they tell the judge what happened by answering questions put to them by the two barristers.

Explain that their evidence is just one part of the case:

> Children sometimes overestimate their roles in a court outcome, feeling
> overly responsible for what happens to the accused. That is why they often

react badly when a case is a not guilty verdict. It's as if they didn't do a good enough job or that the judge did not believe them. Use a puzzle as a visual metaphor for explaining their role in the judge's final decision. Tell them that the judge can only make good decisions about whether somebody has done something wrong if they have all the information from all the witnesses, even the accused if he or she wants to testify. Evidence in court is like pieces of a puzzle. To demonstrate, take a picture or sheet of paper and rip it into six or eight pieces. Lay out the pieces one by one. The police contribute one piece and the other witnesses give other pieces. The child is responsible only for one piece of the entire puzzle.

(PACE UK, no date)

PACE parent support workers have identified eight common anxieties that children and young people have about testifying in cases of CSE.

- Seeing the accused again;

- Not being believed;

- Being in the public eye;

- Being shouted at or told off;

- Feeling responsible for unwanted court outcomes;

- Getting mixed up or forgetting things;

- Crying or getting upset when testifying;

- Talking about sex and genitals in public.

If you can work out what is worrying your child most, you may be able to address their fears and reassure them.

Courts have a Witness Service that should be able to help to prepare the child to give evidence (in some areas there is a specialist Young Witness Service). You can request a visit to the court before the proceedings. This will give the child the opportunity to see for themselves some of the precautions that are offered, such as the chance to give their evidence pre-recorded or via a video link in a different room, security-controlled entry, and so on.

CPS guidance stipulates the need for children to be made aware that the defendant and others in the court room will be able to see them and that if this will cause the child distress (because, for many, fear of being seen by the defendant is worse than fear of seeing the defendant), steps should be taken to address this, such as covering the defendant's monitor.

The child or young person should be given the chance to watch the recording of their ABE interview before their court appearance so as to refresh their memory. This, and then having to see the recording shown in open court, can be very difficult for them, as described by one young person in the research project Making Justice Work:

> You get like reminded and you see yourself, see yourself in that position again. It just reminds you of everything you felt back then. And you feel like degraded, 'cos you don't want people to hear about all that stuff. And you feel embarrassed. You don't want to be reminded. You still think about it and know about it but you don't want to be reminded in that much detail about it, 'cos it just brings it all back.

(Beckett and Warrington, 2015)

The young people in the research expressed serious discomfort with the open nature of the court.

> They talked about feeling intimidated by the presence of the perpetrator's supporters. They also expressed deep discomfort with the fact that strangers, with no connection to their case, could come in and hear intimate details of the abuse they had experienced and queried why greater control could not be exercised over these groups' access to the court:

> 'The public come to court. They show the interview and you don't know who's been looking at it 'cos you're not there, you're not present. It should not be for anyone just to come in. Under 18s should not have an audience 'cos at the end of the day they're a child. They're still kids and this has happened to them and anyone can just walk in and hear it all – it's just stupid!'

(Beckett and Warrington, 2015)

Cross-examination is also a source of anxiety for young people who have to give evidence.

Dealing with the outcome

Prepare the child for both a "guilty" and "not guilty" outcome and explain what "not guilty" and "beyond reasonable doubt" mean:

When an accused is found "not guilty", maybe the jury was 80% sure but that is not enough. "Not guilty" does not mean innocent and it does not mean that people didn't believe the child. The fact that he or she was charged is remembered by the police. A not guilty verdict can often be seen by the child as a very negative outcome. It is important, therefore, to prepare your child for such an outcome, and to always explain this outcome in a more positive manner. You could stress how brave your child has been and how proud you are of them for standing up and telling the truth. Lots of people believed them but the evidence was not strong enough to reach the high level of proof required by the court.

(PACE UK)

Young people interviewed as part of a study on the impact of the criminal justice system (Beckett and Warrington, 2015) said they felt disempowered, isolated and stigmatised by the criminal justice process. They also felt an absence of a sense of justice – particularly where the police or CPS decided there would be no further action, where charges were reduced or dropped (usually without consultation with the young people), where different victims in multiple victim cases received differential treatment and outcomes, and where the young people did not feel the sentences reflected the severity of the crime.

Tragically, the ordeal does not always end even after the court case. Sometimes victims and their families continue to be targeted and stigmatised by certain people in their local communities (such as friends and associates of the perpetrators) even after the case has gone to court and the perpetrators have been found guilty. If this happens, it goes without saying that the police should be informed.

Young people continue to need support whatever the outcome. When the case is over the young person no longer has that focus and they are left feeling empty.

The difficulties of the post court period, and the exacerbating effects of an absence of appropriate support, were also raised by many of the professionals who participated in the research:

'The trial finishes, that's it, police are off. Then the victim is left to be supported by whoever is left and pick the pieces up. There isn't that after care...They are really vulnerable then because they've been victimised because of a vulnerability, they've been through a court process which has then made them vulnerable again and probably re-traumatised them because they've had to go through their experiences in open court. Then it's like, you're on your own. If there is another perpetrator out there or group of perpetrators, it's ideal time, straight after when they're isolated, there is no one there to wrap anything around them, really dangerous time, I think.'

(Beckett and Warrington, 2015)

A striking finding of Making Justice Work is that most of the measures that participants saw as likely to improve young people's negative experiences of criminal justice processes are already recommended or feasible within the current policy and guidance context. They are not, however, being consistently translated into practice. The reasons are many and varied: they include budgetary constraints (and consequent lack of therapeutic support), a lack of compassion and empathy, poor communication and a failure to involve young people in decisions or explain things in ways they could understand. There were examples of good practice but these often rely on an individual's knowledge, understanding or commitment rather than being embedded in a wider professional culture. The researchers say:

This failure to embed humanity within the system has resulted in unnecessary distress, disengagement and re-victimisation.

(Beckett and Warrington, 2015)

5 Understanding the impact of CSE on victims and their families

Why do children so rarely disclose?

There are many reasons why it's fairly rare for children and young people to tell their parents or another adult about the CSE. Many parents feel distressed that their child had been suffering abuse for some time before it was discovered or disclosed.

PACE UK offers some reasons that can prevent children from telling their parents:

- No perception of abuse;
- Belief that the perpetrator is a loving partner;
- Difficulty in talking about sex and sexual relationships;
- Length of time that might have elapsed from the time of abuse;
- Not knowing whom to tell;
- Anxiety, embarrassment and shame;
- Fear of not being believed or of being judged or rejected;
- Fear for personal and family safety;
- Dependency on perpetrators (emotional or for substances);
- A sense of powerlessness and/or isolation;
- Denial ('It happened to someone else');
- Fear of disappointing loved ones;
- Repercussions of crimes they may have been involved in during exploitation;
- Feeling they owe the abuser;

● Hope of rescuing the relationship.

(www.paceuk.info/for-parents/advice-centre/living-with-child-sexual-exploitation/)

Children may not recognise (especially in the grooming phase) that the relationship they are in is abusive. Sometimes they believe the abuser is their boyfriend, who loves them – however badly they are treated. There is a recognised psychological condition called Stockholm Syndrome (see below) in which prisoners and hostages "bond" with their captors.

In some cases, once the abuse begins to escalate, victims may be in a state of fear and helplessness induced by threats, coercion and violence, and feel that there is nothing they can do to get out of the situation.

Perpetrators use a range of methods to control their victims. Sometimes they "normalise" the abuse in their victim's mind so that he or she thinks all relationships must be like this. They will often make threats against the child or their family. Those who have groomed a child online may threaten to disseminate photos or videos the child has sent them (e.g. to post them online).

Perpetrators destroy the child's self-esteem and make the child feel they are to blame or worthless. They may point out that the child accepted certain things in return for sex (e.g. drugs, gifts, money) and make them feel that they were complicit in the abuse. They make the child believe that no-one would listen or believe their story, or that the child would be held responsible and get in trouble for what they have done.

There are additional factors for some children and young people, for example, for boys and those from black and minority ethnic communities.

> *Fears about issues relating to homosexuality are thought to be one of the main reasons boys are reluctant to disclose sexual abuse by men...For black children, dominant racist perspectives of black and minority ethnic sexuality will impact on the child's experience, especially if the sexual abuse is disclosed to someone from outside the community. The child might not want to disclose under these circumstances, or alternatively, these views may confirm the child's own limited experience of the community.*

(Smith, 2015)

In the case of victims from some black and minority ethnic communities, the perpetrator may claim that the victim has brought shame on their family by their behaviour, or that if they report the abuse, this will affect the standing or "honour" of their family.

Recognition, telling and providing help

Dr Carlene Firmin from the University of Bedfordshire's International Centre: Researching Child Sexual Exploitation, Violence and Trafficking has studied the question of child abuse and why children may be reluctant or unable to disclose what is happening to them. Young people are strategic and rational about telling, says Firmin. If they don't think an adult will be able to help, they will decide not to tell. Or if, in previous situations when they have come into contact with professionals they have not perceived them as helpful, this may make them less likely to disclose. They may "test out" a professional by telling them part of what has happened, and decide on the basis of their response whether or not to tell the whole story. It begins with the question of whether they recognise what has happened to them as abuse/exploitation.

Recognition

• No recognition

This is linked to age in that younger children may think abuse is "normal". Peer-to-peer sexual abuse can also be difficult for some children to recognise, because they do not know what "normal" is. In the UK and some other similar Western countries, young people's sexual norms are hugely influenced by their peer group. If sexually harmful relationships are rife within their peer group, the young person may simply assume that "that's how life is".

• Partial recognition

This is an emotional awareness that things are not right, though the child may not yet be able to articulate this to him or herself or to others. They also have no idea how to change the situation.

• Recognition

Recognition may come as a result of receiving help rather than as a precursor to telling – in other words, it is the help and support that allow the young person to finally realise that the situation or relationship they are or have been in is abusive or exploitative. Sometimes recognition is the last thing to happen.

Telling

Disclosure can come about in different ways.

- **Hidden**

Children and young people often actively avoid telling anyone. This may be because they are afraid of the consequences (and they may have been threatened with reprisals). Some have developed a misplaced sense of self-reliance, in which they believe they cannot rely on anyone else and therefore simply don't ask for help.

- **Signs and symptoms**

The child's own behaviour (e.g. signs of stress, distress, anger, "acting out") may give some clues.

- **Prompted telling**

This is when a child discloses their sexual abuse in response to an expression of concern from an adult who has noticed something is wrong – usually someone who knows them well. This may be a teacher or a youth leader, for example. The professional needs to be persistent, but not intrusive, to elicit the child's story.

- **Purposeful**

The child seeks out a professional to tell.

Possible responses from professionals:

Providing help

- No help is offered
- Help related to the child's symptoms is offered (but does not address the underlying cause)

This is often time-limited – for example, school-based counselling or anger management. The child knows they will be offered only six sessions so is unlikely to bring up any serious issues. The opportunity to help them escape from CSE may be missed.

- Help related to the abuse is offered

This is more in-depth support which is not time-limited or limited to the signs and symptoms.

It may be immediate and effective, because it is clear from the start that the child is a victim of CSE. But sometimes the underlying issues of abuse become apparent more gradually.

Sometimes the timing is unfortunate and a lack of flexibility means that young people "age out" of services for under-18s just when they are starting to get help.

(Dr Carlene Firmin, speaking on *Young people's perspectives on abuse and neglect, telling and getting help* at the conference *Safeguarding Adolescents: Emerging evidence, contemporary debates*, November 2016)

Stockholm Syndrome

Some victims' persistent belief that their abuser is someone who loves and cares about them – despite all evidence to the contrary – has been compared to Stockholm Syndrome. In Stockholm in 1973, two criminals took hostages – three women and one man – in a bank and kept them in the bank vault for the next six days with dynamite strapped to their bodies. When they were finally rescued, in spite of the threats and abuse from their captors, the hostages had begun to feel positive towards them. They refused to testify against them in court, and one woman even became engaged to one of her captors.

Psychologists view this emotional bonding with an abuser as a strategy for survival in situations of abuse and intimidation. It is also seen in prisoners of war and cult members, and some writers and researchers have compared it with what happens to women in abusive relationships. The victim is not choosing to take the side of their captor or abuser or adopt their values – rather, their feelings stem from their inherent human need to survive.

There are four situations which can give rise to the development of Stockholm Syndrome. And these also apply in CSE.

- The victim perceives a real threat to their physical or psychological survival.

- There is occasional kindness from the abuser towards the victim.

- The victim is isolated from other people's perspectives by the victim.

- The victim feels unable to escape from the situation.

The victim's overriding concern is to keep the abuser happy, and they base all their decisions on how the abuser will react. They may become angry with anyone who tries to help (including parents and anyone else who tries to rescue them).

The term "trauma bond" is also sometimes used to explain why victims of abuse stay with their abusers. Psychological strategies of denial and distortion mean that victims are unable to evaluate the relationship accurately or to see any way out of it.

The impact of CSE on victims

CSE has a serious impact on many aspects of victims' lives in both the long and the short term, and causes untold damage to their physical, psychological and mental wellbeing and relationships.

Being sexually exploited causes extreme stress, fear, shame, guilt and humiliation; it destroys the child's self-esteem and makes them feel worthless. They are likely to lose sight of and interest in anything that was positive in their lives.

It damages trust and relationships – with parents and siblings, and with other people too. Under the influence of an abuser who tries to get them away from the influence of their parents or carers, they are likely to become hostile, angry and rejecting of them. Victims feel constantly unsafe and that their lives are out of control. They can themselves become controlling of other people in their attempts to avoid anything that could cause "trouble" in their relationship with their abuser or that might anger him. Sometimes families break up under the strain.

Children and young people who have been sexually abused often feel used and dirty. It goes without saying that their ideas and attitudes about sexuality and relationships are likely to be seriously distorted, which could have a damaging long-term impact on their ability to trust anyone or to form healthy, loving, sexual relationships in the future.

> It is possible for a young person who has been sexually abused to become addicted to the heightened arousal the abusive experience produces. They can then feel a physiological need to have sexual contact divorced from any emotional closeness. The young person is also likely to be confused about

their physical feelings and may not label or recognise their sexual feelings as sexual, or may mistakenly label anxiety and fear as sexual feelings.

(Smith, 2015)

There is likely to be a serious impact on their physical health too, with stress-related symptoms such as insomnia, headaches and stomachaches. Some victims experience physical injuries caused by physical and sexual assault and rape, as well as sexually transmitted infections, pregnancy and abortion (sometimes with long-term effects on fertility and childbearing). Some will be introduced to alcohol and drugs by their abusers, and become addicted. Others may self-medicate with drink or drugs to dull the pain they are experiencing. Extreme anxiety and acute distress can result in mental ill-health such as depression, self-harm, eating disorders and suicidal feelings and attempts.

The child or young person is likely to miss school and college (though this is not always the case). Some will skip school to spend time with their abuser, while for others the abuse may be linked to other students or people at school, or to risks outside the school gates. Sometimes staying away can seem like the safest option. Studying seems irrelevant when your life is chaotic and you fear for your safety and that of your family. Motivation to do well or co-operate with teachers disappears. The child's ability to focus on anything else will be severely impacted.

They may be angry and distressed, and express this both in and out of school in ways that get them into trouble. They may become involved in criminal behaviour and end up with a criminal record because of offending linked to their sexual exploitation. Their prospects of doing well at school, college and work are likely to be seriously damaged.

Research into victims of CSE in residential children's homes looked at the children's complex needs and found that as well as the kind of problems outlined above, the staff in the homes noted a number of other vulnerabilities:

- Low self-esteem and poor confidence were ubiquitous across children affected by CSE.

- A lack of insight into their vulnerability and the risks faced was apparent, although respondents could not say whether this was attributable to their youthful sense of invincibility, or a phenomenon specific to this group.

- Children tended to lack any positive friendships or support networks, and had very low expectations of a "good friendship" or of romantic relationships.

- Emotional and communication problems were common, with feelings often communicated through aggression or self-harm.

- Personal hygiene was said to be commonly neglected and could be deliberately used as a barrier.

- Poor diet and neglected health issues were also reported to be common.

(La Valle and Graham, 2016)

Truanting, turning to drink or drugs or running away can make victims more vulnerable to other sexual offenders, even if they have not disclosed the initial sexual exploitation.

Their lives are seriously disrupted and derailed by CSE. Sometimes the consequences include threats to young people's lives and the need to move away from their family to a place of safety. In some cases, even after police involvement, offenders and their associates attempt to continue to intimidate their victims to deter them from going to court.

Many of these vulnerabilities apply to both boys and girls, but boys exploited by males face additional issues:

A boy who has been sexually abused by a man may want to convince himself that he has not been damaged by what would be considered by many to be a homosexual encounter, and he might then become deliberately sexually aggressive towards or preoccupied with females. A boy who has been abused by a man will have to deal with wider society's homophobia, as the shared gender of child and perpetrator often becomes the focus rather than the adult sexual exploitation of the child.

(Smith, 2015)

The impact on families

PACE is the leading national charity working with parents and carers of sexually exploited children, and has a wealth of knowledge about both the impact on families and how professionals can involve families in a positive and constructive way.

Many experience disbelief that their child could be exposed to such a thing without them realising. The trauma and disruption to family life cannot be underestimated. The emotional, mental and physical resilience needed to maintain a job, keep a home routine, control finances and support siblings is significant. Trying to retain a sense of normality, while simultaneously safeguarding a child who is hostile to boundary-setting and will not disclose their whereabouts when missing from home, is extremely challenging. The stress will be compounded should the child face exclusion from school, or is called upon as a witness in a court case.

The strain on parents' own interpersonal relationships can be immense, with many turning to alcohol and/or withdrawing from their partner. Arguments can become a daily feature. Unfortunately, in some families, this rift becomes permanent, with parents separating and one or more of the siblings becoming a looked after child. Many family break-ups occur because parents simply cannot cope with the sense of guilt and shame.

Siblings are also affected by CSE. Some report feeling left out and seek to gain attention in other ways, including the potential for them to become involved in crime or sexual exploitation themselves. Siblings can struggle with the attention that the affected child is receiving, which ultimately leads to a rift in their relationship. In some cases the unaffected child may even ask to be taken into care.

The reality that families can also become crime victims is often overlooked or unknown. They are often subjected to threats, assaults and intimidation by perpetrators. In response, families can be compelled to take extraordinary measures in their attempt to safeguard their child: some uproot the family, moving to another city or even country to get them away from perpetrators. But the stigma associated with sexual exploitation is harder to escape, and its consequences on the child such as anxiety, depression, eating disorders and self-harm can cause enduring misery and isolation for parents and other family members.

(PACE UK, 2014)

Why parents are not "to blame"

There is still a feeling, among the public and perhaps some professionals too, that in some way there must be something dysfunctional about the child's parents or family background if the parents have not been able to prevent their child becoming a victim of CSE. In some cases, of course, victims do come from disadvantaged backgrounds and have chaotic home lives, or are in the care of the local authority. However, many parents of CSE victims are loving, caring, responsible people who would do anything in their power to protect their child from harm. The fact is that exploiters are very skilled at turning the child or young person against their parents and anyone else who might seek to protect them. When a child is in thrall to an exploiter, parents can see their child becoming estranged from them and they feel helpless to do anything about it. They may also feel angry with the child because of what they see as his or her unwillingness to break the bond with their abuser.

Sadly statutory agencies and professionals sometimes wrongly assume that the victim's parents are unwilling, or incapable, of protecting their child from exploitation and therefore they do not involve them, which can lead to parents feeling even more disempowered. Yet the parents are the ones who are in the best position to support the child and help them get out of the situation. In most cases they desperately want to do this.

The relational safeguarding model

The system of "child protection" usually involves protecting a child from risks within the family and home environment. But with CSE, the risk and harm come from people outside the family. So a different model of working with families is needed, and PACE calls this the *relational safeguarding model*. This means professionals working in partnership with parents, facilitating and supporting them, in order to maximise the ability and capacity of both the family and the professionals to safeguard the child.

The relational safeguarding model focuses on:

- maximising the capacity of parents and carers to safeguard their children and contribute to the prevention of abuse and the disruption and conviction of perpetrators;

- early intervention and prevention;

- enabling family involvement in safeguarding processes around the child, including decision making;

- ensuring the safety and wellbeing of the family in recognition of the impact of CSE;

- balancing the child's identity as both an individual and as part of a family unit.

(PACE UK, 2014)

One of the roles of a specialist parents' support worker (see below) is to help parents understand the dynamics of CSE and why their child is behaving this way:

> Improving parental understanding of CSE and the grooming process can break the stranglehold that the perpetrators have on a young person as the parents begin to understand that their child is being manipulated and deliberately being estranged from them. Moreover, some parents need to understand that their child is not responsible for what has happened. This can have a significant effect on family relations and lead to positive change.

(PACE UK, 2014)

6 Supporting CSE survivors and helping them recover

Children and young people need more than a place of safety

Some children and young people who have been sexually exploited come into care as this is seen to be the only way to keep them safe and prevent them from being sexually exploited.

Safety is multi-dimensional, explains Dr Lucie Shuker of the International Centre: Researching Child Sexual Exploitation, Violence and Trafficking, based at the University of Bedfordshire:

> We can disrupt the abuse in the short term by moving the young person out of the area but those relationships will usually be waiting for them when they return. Our research suggests that safety has three dimensions. Firstly, it's physical. We need to make it as hard as possible for perpetrators to access young people whether that's on the phone, online or in person. Secondly, it's relational – we need to make it easier for young people to experience safe and stable relationships that counteract the abuse and to avoid the constant moving between placements that increases the risk of child sexual exploitation. Thirdly, it's got a psychological element too – we need to help young people to find sources of self-identity outside of abusive relationships.

(Shuker, 2015)

Physical, relational and psychological safety are all vital for safeguarding the welfare of young people affected by CSE. Some young people will need a high level of supervision (including with their online activities) to keep them physically safe from perpetrators. But families and carers (in partnership with other professionals) also need to respond to the child's needs for psychological and relational security and to build the child's resilience for what lies ahead.

The right intervention or support needs to be offered at the right time for that individual child.

> *A child-centred approach is needed to recognise which type of security is the first priority for services to work towards for the individual child. For some young people, a stable trusting relationship will be a necessary precondition for attempting to achieve physical safety by disrupting a relationship with a perpetrator. For others in immediate danger, physical safety will be the foundation for work to achieve psychological and then relational security. Crucially, where physical safety is achieved at the expense of relational and psychological security, interventions will only ever be short-term solutions ... and may ultimately hinder exit from exploitative situations or relationships.*

(Shuker, 2013)

The Government agrees that children and young people need a range of other responses as well as a place of safety:

> *Both young people and professionals across a range of studies have indicated that dealing with child sexual exploitation (through approaches such as secure residential units) without providing support to address the interconnected conditions for abuse will be unlikely to provide any long-term change – and, in the short term, could exacerbate their problems leading to increased disengagement from services and increased risk.*

(DfE, 2017, Annex A)

Placement away from home

The placements available to local authorities are not always those best suited to young people's needs. And there is some debate about whether it is always the best response. It causes major disruption to their social and family networks and it can remove them from their supportive family members and other protective adults and friends (if there are any), as well as from the perpetrator.

Researchers for a study for the Department for Education (DfE) note:

> *There is a widely (but not unanimously) held assumption that removing children affected by CSE from their community and placing them in very*

remote areas helps to keep them safe, but there is no evidence to support this.

(La Valle and Graham, 2016)

In some cases, the chance to live somewhere away from the perpetrators is helpful. One child in a specialist foster placement had a history of frequently going missing, using drugs and stealing. However, during the time she was in the placement the police had no cause to see her and she had no contact with exploitative peers and adults she had associated with where she lived before.

Yes, I think location, taking her away from everything that she knew allowed her to step back and reflect on what her behaviours were, what was happening and what it was leading to...She's not displayed any periods where she's gone missing, she's not decided to seek out Facebook or the internet. Helena's (specialist foster carer) been working with her on relationships and all around the issues and things, to give her an understanding of it all, which I think has given her an insight into why we were all worried.

(LA social worker for a child in specialist foster placement, in Shuker, 2013)

Some children and young people will continue to go missing from a foster placement, often to go back and see their family or friends or to be with the perpetrators of the CSE. This understandably causes anxiety for foster carers and social workers. For the professionals, it can be difficult to justify keeping a young person in a foster placement from which they sometimes go missing – rather than moving them to a secure unit – even if moving them does mean disrupting positive relationships they may have developed with their foster carers.

The need for specialist training

It is clear that carers should be given some specialist training for these challenges. But many foster carers are having to manage challenging placements without the necessary training:

A Fostering Network survey of 40 members with experience of looking after children who go missing found that over 50 per cent had not been given training on looking after young people who run away or go missing and concerns were raised about the support they were getting from the local authority.

(Robert Tapsfield, The Fostering Network, oral evidence session to the APPG Inquiry into Children Missing from Care, 2012)

With funding from the DfE, the children's charity Barnardo's has been developing specialist foster care placements for victims of CSE and trafficking. And an increasing number of children's residential homes are beginning to specialise in this kind of placement.

They are not all the "typical" child in care

Not all young people who enter the care system in adolescence primarily because of CSE have what might be considered the typical profile of children in care, and their relationships with their parents are likely to be different too. Researchers who carried out a survey of children's homes for the DfE, looking at approaches to CSE, make the following point:

For those children who entered care in adolescence, relationships with parents may have been strained, but on the whole these children were not in care because of parental neglect or abuse. However, the "coming to light" of the child's sexual exploitation exacerbated any existing parent–child difficulties and could prompt the parents to reject the child, or blame them for what had happened. Respondents believed that CSE had resulted in children completely new to the care system entering residential care, as one explained: 'these are not your typical care kids'.

(La Valle and Graham, 2016)

The power of positive relationships

Whatever the setting, young people need a safe, stable environment where they can feel understood and cared for and not judged for what has happened to them. For some, forming relationships with trusted and caring adults over a period of time is a route to recognising themselves as victims of sexual exploitation – if that has not already happened – and recovering from their traumatic experiences.

Having someone who cares can make all the difference to some children and young people who have experienced sexual exploitation.

In an interview featured on the Barnardo's website, a young man called Joshua credits his CSE worker, John, with turning his life around. Joshua was 14 when his sexual exploitation by older men began. He was in a "sorry state" – but meeting John and talking to him about his experiences, he says, was a turning point.

I had this one person who actually gave a damn what I was going through.

(Barnardo's, no date, *Joshua's Story*)

Most professionals who work in this field agree that "trusted relationships" are crucial to improvements in children's wellbeing. Children and young people feel supported and cared for. But what does it involve? The following description, from Dr Jeannette Cossar, sounds very like what a good foster carer or residential care worker could provide, if they have a good team around them:

- Listening

- Being non-judgemental

- Being honest and transparent

- Being able to repair a relationship when there are ups and downs

- Hanging on in there and making the young person see that you are still there for them and that they are not just a case or just a number

- Being available and accessible

(Jeannette Cossar, Senior Lecturer in the School of Social Work at the University of East Anglia, speaking on *Young people's perspectives on abuse and neglect, telling and getting help at the conference Safeguarding Adolescents: Emerging evidence, contemporary debates*, November 2016)

Barnardo's (2007) advocates the following approach for working with sexually exploited young people:

- Reduce risk;

- Explore strategies with children and young people to help them stay safe in relationships;

- Support them with appointments for sexual health, housing and other services;

- Listen;

- Offer therapeutic/counselling support. Don't judge. Help them access one-to-one support from specialist services;

- Understand needs and risks;

- Assess needs, risk and vulnerability, explore how these can be addressed;

- Advocate;

- Speak up for young people...to other professionals, family members and in meetings, where specialist support services are required;

- Make plans;

- Identify strengths, use young people's ideas, encourage aspirations and interests;

- Offer advice to other professionals, social workers, parents and police, etc;

- Care, worry, encourage and support;

- Be consistent, be tenacious, be there.

Building trust

A proportion of young people who have become victims of CSE are likely to have attachment disorders and feel unloved and unworthy of approval or affection. Somehow foster carers and other workers have to try to forge relationships with them and win their trust and confidence. How can they best do this?

It often takes a long time and is by no means easy. Children and adolescents with highly insecure or disorganised attachment patterns find love scary. Once they have formed a relationship with a caring (non-abusive) adult, they are quite likely to turn against that caring adult and do things to try to make the adult reject them, such as becoming hostile and aggressive.

> Sexual abuse affects a child's capacity to make and sustain relationships. Closeness and intimacy may seem threatening. Adults as protectors may seem an alien concept.

(Smith, 2015)

They may feel angry and antagonistic towards their social worker too, as they feel that this is the person responsible for moving them away from their home and separating them from their family.

Philip Gilligan (2016) conducted research directly with 24 females and one male who were service users of voluntary sector projects in Bradford for those involved in, or at risk of, CSE. He wanted to know what the young women themselves had found helpful in moving on from CSE. They told him that support from a worker who would listen without judgement was crucial. A warm and friendly environment was important, and reliability and flexibility were valued. Mobile phone contact and texting with workers was also highly important for them. Victims need to know that workers 'will be staying around'. The girls mentioned the importance of doing enjoyable activities with workers, with one participant stating 'Just do something with them...to make them feel a bit special...once a month'.

Gilligan also points out the importance of practitioners persevering until victims are ready to engage – it took two years for one young person to trust and be honest with her worker.

Young people may blame themselves for "allowing" the sexual exploitation to happen, or for the fact that they were involved in recruiting others. It can be helpful if carers show the young person that they don't blame them or hold them responsible, and explain that they see their actions in the context of the exploitative, manipulative relationship and the strategies they had to adopt in order to survive.

The process of grooming has been an abuse of trust and the abusive relationship can be a distorted attachment. It should come as no surprise that young people who have been sexually exploited would be mistrustful of adults, even those who want to support them.

Relationship-based practice and being child-centred

Relationship-based practice involves getting to know the child and listening to them rather than simply going in with your own agenda. If they see you as a person who has been willing to listen to them, this can help when you have to have difficult conversations.

Practitioners and carers need to develop ways to work with children and young people who have experienced CSE without insisting to them that they are "victims" and must "disclose" their CSE before they can get any help.

It requires great sensitivity on everyone's part. It also requires patience. As the Scottish Government urges:

> Care must... be taken not to simply dismiss children's perspectives on events in our attempts to help them begin to understand the abusive nature of their experiences, as this can consolidate harm and vulnerability. In line with GIRFEC (Getting It Right For Every Child) principles, it is imperative that this work is undertaken in partnership with children, in a safe environment and at a pace that is appropriate for them – this frequently means the provision of long-term support. It is also imperative that such work is holistic, addressing the vulnerability and risk factors that contributed to the abuse in the first place rather than simply closing down avenues of contact.

(Beckett and Walker, 2016)

CSE does not define a young person

You will need to get to know the child placed with you as a person, not just as a CSE victim. They don't want to be – and shouldn't be – defined by what has happened to them. They may well not want to talk about the CSE – certainly not at first – and some may not even see it as a big deal:

> None of the young people say CSE is their priority. They have multiple problems. They say: 'CSE is the least of my problems, but it's all that you lot want to talk about.'

(Nicholas Marsh, Operational Development Lead, Achieving Change Together, speaking at the Children & Young People Now conference *Tackling Child Sexual Exploitation: Prevention and Protection*, December 2016)

As well as being CSE victims, they are still teenagers with all the physical and neurological changes and social preoccupations that are features of the teenage years. That means:

- An increased focus on their identity – who are they really?;
- Sensitivity to their "status" among their peer group;
- Self-consciousness about how they are perceived by others;
- The opinions and norms of their friends and peers can be more influential than those of parents, carers and other adults;

- Their emotions and moods can be intense and volatile;

- They desire independence and want to be treated as an adult yet at other times feel like a child;

- They seek excitement, are impulsive and willing to take risks (and may even seek them out);

- They may not be interested in planning for the future and/or looking beyond the short term.

The early days of placement

The child or young person may arrive in a traumatised state, having had to leave their home and family, perhaps unwillingly. The first priority is to help them feel safe. It is only when children feel safe and have stabilised that the "real" work of helping them can start. This can take some time.

It goes without saying that your home – whether it's a foster placement or a residential children's home – will feel different in every sense from the home they have been brought up in. The culture and dynamics of your family (or children's home) will be very different from what they are used to. They are likely to feel uncomfortable at first, however welcome you try to make them.

Some children's homes are completely off the beaten track geographically – the thinking behind this is to provide a kind of sanctuary where it is not easy for abusers to reach the young people, or vice versa. But of course to the young person the placement may feel more like being sent into exile rather than a sanctuary.

A lot of looked after young people feel almost forced into an alien culture which they haven't chosen, in a place they haven't chosen. They have no power or control – they are powerless and out of control. They've been coerced on many levels – by the State as well as what's gone on before.

(Stuart Hannah, North Leeds Psychotherapy Services, personal communication, 2016)

The first few days are likely to be spent getting to know the young person (without overwhelming them with questions, of course) and helping them to feel safe. Work out what will make them feel comfortable in your home and family. Find out about them: what do they like to eat, what football team do they support, how do they like to do their hair, what kind of music do they like, what would they like to do if they ever won the lottery?

You'll need to gauge when they are starting to feel they can cope with "normal" life.

> The first stage is stabilisation, bringing in the ordinary. Do they feel ready to start at a new school or college? Do they feel ready for anything other than just being looked after for a few days or weeks? What level of attention isn't going to feel too intrusive for them? You need to stay close but not so close that they feel overwhelmed or irritated. These are young people who are relationally very shut down.

(Stuart Hannah, North Leeds Psychotherapy Services, personal communication, 2016)

In the early days of the placement and especially if young people are placed away from their own area, they could spend some time waiting for a school or college place to be arranged. So foster carers need to fill this time with activities that will appeal to the young people, to try to prevent them from getting bored and being drawn back to risky behaviour.

Countering the continuing "pull" of the perpetrators

As a foster carer or residential care worker looking after a child or young person who has been sexually exploited, you will of course be aware of the risk that the young person may try to contact the perpetrator(s) and the precautions that need to be in place.

It can be hard to understand why some young people continue to be drawn towards the person or people who are (or have been) sexually exploiting them.

For some young people, their childhood experiences have given them few inner resources to draw on when they are bored or their life seems dull and uneventful:

> We need to understand that a lot of young people have such low self-esteem that their approach is that bad drama is better than no drama, so given the choice of staying in yet again by themselves, or going to that flat although they know some dodgy things happen there, they are going to go to the flat because at least someone wants them to be there.

(Richard Haigh, Programme Manager, The Children's Society, in an oral evidence session to the APPG Inquiry into Children Missing from Care, 2012)

Carers need to show that they want to spend time with the young person. In the recent past, it may have been only the abuser who made them feel wanted. The challenge is to make their new environment somewhere they want to be.

You have to be more attractive than the alternative. What's attractive enough about you or your home or your family to make them want to hang out with you rather than their peers? It might be your food, your sense of humour, or you play football, or you like the same music.

At some point they may be ready to make new friends. But if they can't stand you, they won't be interested in anyone you introduce them to – such as those nice, well-functioning, capable kids who are so fundamentally different from them.

Making contact with those people (i.e. the perpetrators) might seem preferable to the nice cosy alternative. They are so familiar with that other world.

(Stuart Hannah, North Leeds Psychotherapy Services, personal communication, 2016)

I used to be on the run like every day. I used to think 'Just do it, you only live once'. Now I'd think 'I've got a bed in there! I ain't got a bed out there'. Or 'It's warm in here, and I got dinner sitting on the side', something like that.

(Girl in specialist foster placement quoted in Shuker, 2013)

Carers need to try to get the child to stay and invest in the placement rather than running away to get back home or back to their abusers. At various stages the child's reason to stick around will vary, say researchers who looked at specialist foster placements:

In the early days this could be involving the young person in fun and engaging activities. In the medium to long term it was more likely to be a warm environment where they were well supported and cared for, and had opportunities to belong and succeed.

(Shuker, 2015)

Responding therapeutically

What's sometimes called a "strengths-based" approach can be helpful.

> *In essence this means to focus on the strengths and resources of the individual, rather than concentrating only on the problems and difficulties. It is all too easy for adults to become preoccupied with the problem, rather than seeing the young person in the round. In this way the interests, motivations, resources and capacities of the young person get pushed to one side. To use a strengths-based approach involves a shift in perspective. Look for the strengths, and see how you can build on those.*

(Coleman, 2016)

Young people in these placements are very sensitive to other people's judgement of them – they are likely to feel shame and humiliation and wonder what people think. So it's important for foster carers and residential workers to be non-judgemental.

Many young people are confused about "consent" and may feel that because they co-operated with the perpetrator while under the influence of alcohol or drugs or because of threats, they somehow gave their consent to what happened. These issues will be addressed in therapy they have with specialist sexual exploitation workers or psychotherapists, but as a foster carer or other care worker, you can ensure that you give the child the same message about the impact of grooming and about predatory adults who leave children with little or no means of escape.

You can of course provide a listening ear if the young person wants to talk about it, or you may be able to communicate it more obliquely, for example, by discussing storylines in soaps that you watch together, or events in the news.

Children's emotional responses

There are a few things carers need to be aware of when looking after children and young people who have had traumatic experiences.

Sometimes, after trauma, people get flashbacks so that for a moment they feel as though they are back in the situation and relive their terrifying experiences – they appear to be cut off or dissociated from the world around them, losing awareness of their surroundings for a short time. Night terrors are a kind of flashback that occur in sleep.

Another feature of trauma is that certain stimuli such as a smell, a taste, a sound – for instance, a particular piece of music – or a place or type of place that was associated with their experiences can trigger memories and lead to flashbacks or emotional distress.

Children and young people "acting out" their feelings (expressing their distress, anger and shame by aggressive, destructive or violent behaviour or self-harm) is something of which most foster carers and residential workers will be aware and have experience. It will be helpful for the young person if you can help them identify what is making them feel angry or distressed, recognise possible triggers and come up with strategies they can use to feel safer and to express their feelings in safer ways (the therapist may also be addressing these issues).

You can try to be a resource for the child when they are agitated, angry or upset. Over a period of time, as you get to know and understand them, you may be able to help them to calm down and recognise and express their feelings in other ways, such as sharing their feelings with you or a friend, punching pillows, listening to music or playing music, going to the gym or going for a run or walk together.

> *Healing and recovery work can happen in different ways and places, not just with a professional therapist. Remember you are teaching your child to learn to take care of themselves, to be able to get help when they need it and to use it effectively.*
>
> (Smith, 2015)

Rebuilding lives

Once young people have settled into the placement, they can return to education. In some children's residential homes, education may be provided at the home. For those in foster care, starting at a new mainstream school or college can be challenging but it can also be a positive thing to make a new start and make up for lost time. As with other children and young people in foster care, they may want to have in mind a "cover story" to tell their new friends rather than disclose the reason they are in foster care, in case this is used negatively against them.

Foster carers and residential care workers can encourage young people to learn new skills, to do tasks that will prepare them for independence such as cooking and washing clothes, and to take up new hobbies. There are likely to be glitches along the way, of course.

It is important to consider what happens when risky behaviour does happen. How does the adult respond? If the adult can find ways of managing their emotions, and remain calm and supportive, this will help enormously. A young person in foster care is only too likely to interpret criticism as rejection. If the adult can make it clear that they will remain supportive, even if the young person has messed up, this can have a big impact on future relationships.

(Coleman, 2016)

What do foster carers need to make a success of a CSE placement?

These children need intensive support from their carers. It's a role that's certainly not for everyone. Who is suitable? Researchers identified five areas that were relevant to the role of being a specialist foster carer for sexually exploited and trafficked young people:

- Parenting personality (their confidence, commitment, compassion and ability to cope);

- Level of support given to carers, especially in the early stages when safety measures were being negotiated and carers often needed quick answers and advice when they were unsure of how to manage certain situations;

- Experience in fostering teenagers helped but was not necessary or sufficient on its own;

- Training – the carers felt that specialist training had helped prepare them;

- Availability – at least one carer needed to be available full-time, particularly in the early days of the placement.

(Adapted from Shuker, 2013)

Therapeutic interventions

In an ideal world, every child or young person who has been a victim of CSE would be offered support from a specialist practitioner or therapist. They may be offered therapeutic work such as specialist counselling or psychotherapy to help them deal with their emotional distress. They should also have some psycho-educational work to understand the nature of CSE and how to stay safe in future. Sometimes creative therapies such as art and drama are offered too. These can be provided by a range of practitioners from the statutory or voluntary sectors.

Some children's symptoms are so extreme and their behaviours so concerning that they may need psychiatric assessment and intervention. Some will need longer-term psychotherapy. In terms of the evidence base, trauma-based cognitive behavioural therapy has been found to be helpful with a range of symptoms, such as post-traumatic stress disorder, depression, behaviour problems, feelings of shame and so on. But a range of therapeutic interventions can be used, either one-to-one or in a group setting.

Issues around confidentiality will need to be addressed both with the child's social worker and with you as the child's primary caregiver.

> Therapy should be a special time for the child. It is private and what is shared between the child and their helper is confidential. However, if the child or young person wants to share the contents of their therapy sessions, they should be able to do so...If the child is in a group, they will have to recognise the need to respect other group members' privacy...
>
> However, it needs to be made clear from the beginning what information is private and what will be shared with the adults who have a responsibility to protect the child or young person. Generally, anything that would indicate the child is going to harm themselves or cause harm to others should be shared outside the session.
>
> (Smith, 2015)

You and/or the professional who referred the child for therapy may also be given some feedback regarding the sessions, and the therapist is likely to discuss this "progress report" with teenagers before talking to you.

Be aware that when therapy starts and the child begins to discuss what has happened to them, "difficult behaviour" may get worse before it gets better. However:

> If, as a primary caregiver, you feel the treatment is doing more harm than good, it is very important to discuss this with the professional helper as soon as possible.
>
> (Smith, 2015)

Sometimes additional work will need to be done with the child or young person, for example, to prepare them for giving evidence in legal proceedings or to prepare them for a move to residential care.

Pre-trial therapy and counselling

It seems therapy is not always offered, perhaps due to the fear that in court the defence could claim the child has somehow been "coached" by the therapist and that this could compromise the child's evidence.

> *The CPS guidance...is clear that the best interests of the victim or witness are the paramount consideration in decisions about therapy. There is no bar to a victim seeking pre-trial therapy or counselling and neither the police nor the CPS should prevent therapy from taking place prior to a trial.*

(Crown Prosecution Service, 2013)

The CPS says that if there is a demonstrable need for therapy and it is possible that the therapy will prejudice the criminal proceedings, consideration may need to be given to abandoning those proceedings in the interests of the child's wellbeing.

The types of support available vary according to the services provided locally (e.g. local authority, health or voluntary sector organisations). Officers need to know what is available in their area.

> *Where investigators know the victim is seeing a therapist or counsellor, they should brief the therapist or counsellor at an early stage to inform them about the court process and their disclosure obligations.*

(College of Policing, 2017)

But in practice this doesn't always happen. Making Justice Work, an investigation (Beckett and Warrington, 2015) into the experiences of criminal justice for children and young people victimised through sexual exploitation, gathered the views of a number of young people and concluded that all too often, the investigative and prosecution needs were prioritised over the victim's welfare needs. Young people's needs for advocacy and therapeutic support – both pre-trial and post-trial or if the case was dropped – often went unmet.

> *The importance of pre-trial therapy was reiterated by several professional participants who also noted difficulties accessing this for the young people*

they were working with. A number of potential reasons were identified for this including: capacity/resourcing issues, confusion about what is, and isn't allowed and, associated to this, reluctance on the part of some providers to take on therapeutic support when there are legal proceedings pending.

(Beckett and Warrington, 2015)

One professional told the researchers:

'Some of these children are absolutely on their knees they're so traumatised, and to stop them from having therapy for at least a year while something goes to prosecution – that's wrong.'

As well as pre-trial therapy, if the perpetrators are not convicted some young people are likely to need support from their carers and other professionals to help them cope with their anger, frustration and sense of betrayal about them "getting away with it".

Teamwork in foster care

Foster carers do not work alone, of course. They are very much part of a team of professionals supporting the child and of course they have a supervising social worker to support them. How does all this look in practice? Here's an example:

Sadia had been placed in foster care, following the breakdown of her relationship with her family. She was found by professionals to be at high risk of child sexual exploitation due to the people she was associating with. Sadia was finding it very difficult to come to terms with her feelings of rejection by her family and had started to misuse alcohol as she felt it helped her manage her emotions and feelings. She was also desperate to be accepted. As a result of this, she committed a minor offence with a new friend. The workers responsible for Sadia (a social worker, a youth offending team worker, her foster carer and the CAMHS worker) understood how her sense of rejection, alcohol use and need to be wanted made her highly vulnerable and increased the risk of exploitation.

In order to reduce this risk, the workers focused on developing a good relationship with Sadia and introducing her to new friends. She worked with the CAMHS worker to develop better ways of coping with her sense of rejection. Sadia responded very well to this approach, stopped misusing alcohol and had not reoffended. Her youth offending team worker understood that any potential reoffending was linked to her emotional needs and, by supporting the work of other partners to address these needs, addressed her offending behaviour. The workers took a considered and sensitive approach to the work. Sadia was not overwhelmed by the number of professionals involved and understood why she needed support. As her emotional well-being improved, she made new friends. The risk of child sexual exploitation was managed well.

(HMIP, HMIC, CQC, Ofsted, 2016)

Providing support in residential children's homes

A report for the Department for Education (La Valle and Graham, 2016) looked at the tailored support provided to children affected by CSE who are placed in residential care. This study aimed to identify approaches used in children's homes, explore their benefits and analyse what seems to work well. The researchers' findings on effective practice in children's homes have some messages that will resonate with foster carers as well as residential care staff. It's well worth reading the full report, especially if you work in a residential children's home.

None of the homes collected information on children's outcomes after they left the setting. So, while homes reported positive outcomes for children, there is no systematic evidence to confirm these benefits and how long they last after the child leaves.

The package of support that the children's homes were providing to children affected by CSE reflects the range of complex needs that these children had. To a large extent, these were the kind of services (for example, education, health, recreational activities, therapy) provided for those suffering from trauma, with the addition of specific CSE educational programmes.

Recognising themselves as victims

The aims of the children's homes were similar, regardless of which model of working they used.

The ultimate aim was that children recovered from CSE, the risk of CSE was eliminated or greatly reduced, and they could have a more "normal" life going forward. To reach those aims, children needed to achieve a series of incremental steps and understand that they had been exploited. The recognition of CSE was seen as an enormous breakthrough, and achieving it relied on several factors, including: beginning to value themselves; comprehending "consent"; appreciating the components of healthy friendships and relationships; learning how to keep safe; and no longer desiring contact with the perpetrators.

…Interviewees stressed that this process was neither simple nor linear. Individual children had their own timeframe; "stages" were interdependent and overlapped, and regression was common.

(La Valle and Graham, 2016)

Another major milestone was developing an understanding of grooming and the concept of "consent", with children and young people finally realising that they had not in fact freely consented to what had been done to them. Staff helped them to see that, for example, dressing in a certain way or accepting gifts did not amount to consent, and that the effects of drugs and alcohol undermined the validity of any consent.

Here are some of the main points about what makes for effective practice in supporting children affected by CSE. The researchers point out that this largely reflects the evidence on what underpins good residential practice more generally, although some additional dimensions and adaptations were identified as important. There were no quick fixes, and work with some young people could take months or years. The longer the CSE had gone on, the longer it would take for the child to recover.

- Good residential practice is strongly dependent on staff's skills, attitudes and consistency, and on staff having sufficient time to dedicate to children and the ability to work therapeutically with them. However, the additional CSE training and input from specialist staff on CSE-related issues was seen as very important.

- Effective residential practice is also underpinned by good interagency work…particularly relevant to CSE were joint protocols and information-sharing in relation to missing children, and identifying and prosecuting CSE perpetrators. Specialist external agencies also seem to play an important role in delivering CSE educational programmes in residential settings.

- Children's meaningful involvement in decisions that affect their lives is a basic right…the opportunity to become "active agents" can help to support a sense of self that is apart from victimhood, and develop self-confidence and self-efficacy. As well as from a range of mechanisms used in residential care to involve children, the literature indicates that opportunities for children to provide mutual support around CSE could be very empowering. This was done through group work around CSE, and in one programme identified in the literature, CSE survivor mentors provided support to their peers who had been sexually exploited.

- Working with the families of children in residential care is an important but often neglected aspect of good residential practice. For children affected by CSE, family work needs to consider the difficulties families may be facing in accepting and understanding what has happened to their children, as well as the fact that some families may be posing or contributing to CSE risks.

- The sustainability of the improvements made while in residential care was also seen as being crucially dependent on the transition arrangements out of residential care.

(La Valle and Graham, 2016, pp7–8)

Not always a happy outcome

For some young people, it can take years before they learn to trust new adults. The suffering, pain and the betrayals they have experienced can sometimes make this almost impossible. Sadly, foster carers and care workers won't always be able to turn around the life of a troubled and traumatised teenager. Some placements break down quickly. With others, even if carers and others do everything in their power to help, the placement does not always succeed in helping the child to recover and move on.

Some young people will continue to show symptoms of extreme psychological distress and/or mental illness. Some will go on to spend time in psychiatric hospitals and/or in secure accommodation or prison, and some tragically take their own lives.

My experience of teenagers with trauma is that some of them are completely unreachable and always will be...There will be sad, tragic stories in the lives of these foster families.

You have to try. If opening your home and your hearts and your lives to this needy, vulnerable group of children is your vocation, then you must have got there somehow – and these children do need that unconditional love.

(Stuart Hannah, North Leeds Psychotherapy Services, personal communication, 2016)

Secondary trauma

Living with children and young people who have had such terrible experiences and witnessing the damage it has done to them is not easy. It can be stressful and upsetting work, as well as sometimes very worrying if children run away, for example, or if they fear for their lives. Child sexual exploitation can take its toll on people who care about the victims, as well as the victims themselves.

Secondary trauma is a condition that can affect those who look after and emotionally support other people who have experienced trauma. When you empathise with a child and "feel their pain" you can absorb something of the power and intensity of the child's emotional distress, which can have a negative impact on your own mental health and wellbeing. Symptoms can include sleeplessness, exhaustion, social withdrawal, avoidance and feelings of guilt. It can be hard for the person affected by secondary trauma to recognise it in themselves.

Awareness of the possibility of secondary trauma and good supervision from a supervising social worker can go some way towards ensuring it is recognised and that the carer gets some support and can think about ways to relieve the stress.

7 Keeping children safe

Whether in foster care, kinship care, a residential children's home or a secure unit, one of the main purposes of placing young people away from home is to keep them safe from contact with their perpetrators. Such contact poses a risk that sexual exploitation could continue or start again, or that perpetrators might intimidate them to prevent them from giving evidence in court. The issues of psychological and relational safety are addressed in chapter 6.

Issues around safety that must be managed by carers in all types of setting include: preventing children and young people from running away, keeping perpetrators away from them – both online and in the real world – and teaching them to recognise and manage risks. Some of the ways of doing this are common to all settings, but some are specific to particular settings.

Safety in children's residential homes

In the children's home setting, according to researchers (La Valle and Graham, 2016), safety underpinned all the work that the homes did.

Detailed risk assessments were developed when children arrived, and were regularly monitored and reviewed. Key messages about recognising risks and keeping safe were reinforced through specific work, as well as informally through the home's everyday activities, such as discussing relevant storylines from TV programmes. When children went missing, discussions were held on their return, to explore what factors had prompted them to run away and what could have been done differently, and to get them to understand the actual and potential consequences of their actions.

Some measures, aimed at keeping children safe, were found to be common to all the homes in this study:

- providing high levels of staff supervision;
- limiting and/or monitoring access to phones, internet and money;
- locating homes in "safe", usually remote, areas;
- reward and sanction systems;

- physically restraining children in very extreme circumstances.

The homes in the study accepted children with serious absconding behaviour linked to CSE, and the main strategy to ensure their immediate safety was a high level of supervision.

> *Commonly, one or even two members of staff were allocated to the child, all day and at night. Staff chaperoned children when they went out, and followed them when they tried to leave on their own without permission. The aim was for this very high level of supervision to be gradually reduced in line with a child's progress in understanding and managing risks.*

> *...Phones and internet access can represent major risks for children affected by CSE, and access to these was closely monitored and restricted, mainly to prevent children from contacting their exploiters. Practices varied. In secure and some non-secure homes, no mobile phones were allowed, supervised calls could only be made from the home's landline, and the internet could only be accessed for school work and under staff supervision. In other settings, the aim was to gradually increase unsupervised access to phones, the internet and social media, as these are currently part of every child's life and children needed to learn to use them safely. However, use was very closely supervised (e.g. staff checked call records and children's social media accounts, mobile phones were kept in the office overnight). If children put themselves at risk through access to the phone and internet, restrictions were re-imposed and additional work done on using these safely. Access to money was also closely monitored. While work was done to teach children to manage budgets, staff had to ensure that this was done safely and money was not used to put themselves at risk, for example, by buying a mobile phone.*

> (La Valle and Graham, 2016, pp29–30)

A key successful outcome was when children accepted their own vulnerability and stopped trying to run away:

> *Children often had little appreciation of their own vulnerability to multiple dangers, such as perpetrators, including traffickers, finding and taking a child, or being attacked or taken advantage of in other ways besides CSE. When homes were in very remote areas, running away brought additional risks of physical injury or exposure. The shift towards this outcome came when children showed that they desired to, and had some understanding of, how to keep themselves safe. Fundamental to this was reduced absconding...*

Many examples were given of children who had absconded frequently or constantly in previous placements, but had had fewer or no missing incidents, or attempts to run away, in the current home. The children were reported as saying that this resulted from feeling safe, loved and cared for in the home, as well as becoming aware of their vulnerability. As one interviewee put it, the aim was that the "external boundaries" initially imposed by the home became internalised so that the child knew how to, and wanted to, keep themselves safe.

(La Valle and Graham, 2016, p16)

Safety in foster placements

Fostering young people who have experienced CSE presents particular challenges – the stakes are so high, and the precautions more difficult to implement in a family home compared with a residential placement.

The carer will need a safety plan that has been worked out by them and the young person's social worker, their supervising social worker and possibly also the police. In some cases, the young person's school might also need to be a partner in the safety plan; for instance, they could be made aware that he or she must not use social networking sites while in school.

Ideally there will also be input from the young person too. You will obviously explain to them why there's a need for rules and boundaries – to keep them safe in future – and what the sanctions will be. In an ideal world this would be achieved via discussion and negotiation rather than imposition, but that may not always be possible.

A study of specialist foster care provided by Barnardo's (Shuker, 2013) reported on the safety precautions taken by foster carers. The strategies adopted depended on both the particular young person's level of risk and need, and the professional opinions and policies of those supporting the placements.

For example, some carers would not lock the front door at night or during the day, even if there was a high risk of the young person going missing, while others would. Some judged that it was safer to make sure the young person always had credit on their phone in case they were in trouble, while in a number of placements young people had no access to a phone in case they used it to contact those who posed a risk to them.

In some placements young people had no access to the internet, no direct access to money, and were accompanied everywhere they went. The length of time such measures were applied varied, but they were often relaxed within a few weeks or months, if it was felt that the young person was now at lower risk of harm, and to allow the young person the opportunity to show they had understood the risks and could manage their own behaviour.

(Shuker, 2013)

The young person may rage against the rules and boundaries, of course. Their life when they were being sexually exploited was chaotic but consistency in rules and boundaries sends an important message that they are now safe and contained:

You are communicating to the child that there is control in the home, that the foster carer is not going to be overwhelmed and can implement these safety measures. There's a predictability and a consistency that actually creates a sense of safety. It's challenging but not impossible.

(Lucie Shuker, International Centre: Researching Child Sexual Exploitation, Violence and Trafficking, personal communication, 2017)

Safety on the internet

Use of the internet and mobile phones is, of course, a huge issue for carers of children and young people who have been sexually exploited. Children and young people come into care from challenging backgrounds where, in some cases, their parents have taken little or no interest in their online activities, where there have been few rules and boundaries around their online behaviour, and where they have had poor role models.

They are separated from their family and friends, as well as the perpetrators, and taking away their mobile phone or internet access to stop them making contact with the perpetrators is not likely to go down well.

A determined young person may be keen to find ways to make contact with family members and other people they are not meant to be in touch with. For others – who may be afraid of being traced by their abusers – there's a risk of inadvertently giving away their location if they use location-sharing websites and features such as digital photos, geolocation and "find my friends" apps on smartphones. This could potentially lead to abusers or traffickers knowing where they are living. So foster carers and young people themselves need to be aware of these risks and what to do to guard against them.

Because of the safety plan, foster carers should be clear about what the child is and isn't allowed in terms of social networking, internet use and mobile phones, and what level of supervision is needed for the child. More stringent measures are likely to be used where children and young people are known to have been victims of CSE (or at high risk) compared with other placements.

In these placements, where young people's safety is at risk and could be so easily compromised, it may well be that (at least at first) young people are not allowed to use the internet or their mobile phones (though this would not be good practice in an "ordinary" foster placement). Monitoring what the child is saying and with whom they are communicating online would similarly not normally be appropriate in foster care but may well be justified in cases such as these where the risk is high.

When a young person is allowed access to the internet (for example, for homework) the foster carers are likely to need to supervise them at all times. If it is decided at some point that the young person should be allowed some access without supervision, the carers need to have in place precautions such as setting passwords, monitoring their activity, using parental controls and "safe search", limiting access to certain sites or using security settings on routers to prevent children from accessing the internet when they are not allowed to, for instance at night.

Of course young people may be able to find ways to get around all of these precautions, whether by being technically very capable or by finding friends at school who will let them use their mobile phones. But it is important to do everything you can.

> The message that's being communicated – even if it's impossible to enforce at some points – is 'I'm not so scared of the internet that I'm not going to try and make you safe'.

(Lucie Shuker, International Centre: Researching Child Sexual Exploitation, Violence and Trafficking, personal communication, 2017)

These technological measures are not the only way to protect children from online risk. The way children use social networking and the internet is a reflection of what's going on in their lives and in their heads. So it is not all about understanding the technology – far from it. Getting through to the young person about the need to keep themselves safe from risky people is a key part of this, although it will take time for them to understand and accept this message.

Young people will eventually need to be given the opportunity to use the internet and social networking again, even if it is withdrawn for a time. The child's social worker and the supervising social worker also need to support foster carers with the complex task of striking the right balance. And above all, the young person needs to *want* to keep safe and avoid being targeted and groomed again. This is all part of the recovery process.

Some of the specialist foster carers in the Barnardo's study had done impressive work in getting online safety messages across to the young people:

> There were some very clear examples of times when Shauna had responded
> in really positive ways to keep herself safe. So as an example, somebody had
> contacted Shauna via the internet, and the carer had found the chat log and
> Shauna had responded to that person, 'I'm 13, you know that I'm younger
> and you know you shouldn't be contacting me' and then she'd ended that
> conversation.

(Barnardo's project worker, quoted in Shuker, 2013, p79)

In another case, while making a collage illustrating how she would say "no" to "wrong things" since being in foster care, the child commented:

> Saying 'No' to like, let's say you met someone off the internet, you never met
> them, they go 'Let's meet in a pub' and it's like nine o'clock at night. Like
> back then I would have been 'Yeah all right' but now I'd be like, 'Mate it's nine
> o'clock at night, I don't know who you are'.

(Child quoted in Shuker, 2013, p90)

Some foster carers are very confident about measures they can take to keep children online and/or monitor what they are doing. But there are still many who lack the knowledge, skills and confidence they need to engage with this and who need more training and support from their agencies.

There is a huge amount of help and advice online for parents and carers about how to reduce online risk and get safety messages across to children and teenagers. A number of excellent websites provide information for parents and carers, as well as resources – video films, games and so on – that they can use alongside their child to educate them about the risks. The NSPCC also provides an online course for people working with children and young people. See *Further reading and resources* for a list of useful resources.

What about the future?

Eventually young people need to move on from the setting where they have been placed. As they progress they may be able to move from a secure centre to a children's home, from a children's home to a foster placement or into semi-independent living, or from a foster placement to independence – or, of course, they may be able to return home from any of these settings. But these transitions need careful planning and support if the improvements that have been achieved are to be sustained – this is particularly vital, of course, if they are returning home to the neighbourhood where the sexual exploitation took place.

Unfortunately, planning for the future and long-term support are sometimes lacking.

In June 2015, as part of a pilot project, a specialist house was opened in Durham to accommodate and provide therapeutic support to young people who had been sexually exploited. Aycliffe Secure Centre CSE Innovation Project was funded by the Department for Education and developed in partnership with Barnardo's and the Odysseus mentoring project. Well-supported transitions were seen as vital and workers who had developed relationships with young people were going to provide ongoing support through their transitions into the community.

Teenagers from 13 to 17 were referred, mainly on three-month orders (with some extended to six months). However, rather than coming mainly from the North-East, referrals came from much further afield and this made it much more difficult to provide "throughcare support".

The evaluation found that:

> ...Staff succeeded in developing some very positive relationships. There was some evidence of improvements in the mental and emotional wellbeing of some young people during their time at Aycliffe. However, the project has been unable to address the complex underlying difficulties...in the short time available to do so. In most cases, positive transitions into suitable placements were not achieved. Local authority planning was poor and placements difficult to find.

(University of Bedfordshire and NatCen Social Research, 2016, available at http://springconsortium.com/wp-content/uploads/2016/11/Durham-Aycliffe-Evaluation-Summary-v2.pdf)

The researchers say that a placement needs to be part of an integrated long-term plan by the placing authority and point out that a secure placement, however good, cannot positively affect outcomes in the absence of long-term solutions. Obviously this is out of the hands of foster carers and residential care workers, however.

The level of supervision that is possible in secure or semi-secure units cannot continue forever. When children move out of secure or semi-secure homes, staff want to be confident that they will still be safe:

...all the risk anxieties relevant to CSE became more heightened when a move to a less intensive setting or back to the family home was expected. For example, how far were the children able to appreciate risk, use social media safely and avoid cultures and situations which could re-expose them to risk? How likely were they to re-contact, or be contacted by, the perpetrators?

(La Valle and Graham, 2016, p47)

All you can do as a foster carer or residential care worker is give the best care you can for as long as the child is with you, providing a safe place and some stability after the traumatic experiences they have endured. Your compassion, empathy and support will build their self-esteem, resilience and strength and help them to see the future as a more hopeful place.

References

All Party Parliamentary Group (APPG) for Runaway and Missing Children and Adults and the APPG for Looked after Children and Care Leavers (2012) *Report from the Joint Inquiry into Children who go Missing from Care,* London: APPG

Barnardo's (2007) *Bwise2 Sexual Exploitation: A preventative education pack for use with 12 to 17-year-olds in pupil referral units, residential units and schools,* London: Barnardo's

Barnardo's (2011) *Puppet on a String: The urgent need to cut children free from sexual exploitation,* London: Barnardo's

Barnardo's (no date) *Joshua's Story,* available at: www.barnardos.org.uk/what_ we_do/our_work/sexual_exploitation/about-cse/cse-greg/cse-relationships. htm

Barnardo's (no date) *Nadine's Story,* available at: www.barnardos.org.uk/what_ we_do/our_work/sexual_exploitation/about-cse/cse-greg/cse-relationships. htm

Barnardo's (no date) *Samuel's Story,* available at: www.barnardos.org.uk/what_ we_do/our_work/sexual_exploitation/about-cse/cse-greg/cse-relationships. htm

Beckett H (2011) *'Not a world away': The sexual exploitation of children in Northern Ireland,* Belfast: Barnardo's Northern Ireland

Beckett H, Brodie I, Factor F, Melrose M, Pearce J, Pitts J, Shuker L and Warrington C (2013) *"It's wrong – but you get used to it": A qualitative study of gang-associated sexual violence towards, and exploitation of, young people in England,* University of Bedfordshire

Beckett H, Holmes D and Walker J (2017) *CSE: Definition and guide for professionals: extended text,* Luton: University of Bedfordshire

Beckett H and Walker J (2016) *Child Sexual Exploitation Definition and Practitioner Briefing Paper,* Edinburgh: Scottish Government

Beckett and Warrington C (2015) *Making Justice Work: Experiences of criminal justice for children and young people affected by sexual exploitation as victims and witnesses,* Luton: University of Bedfordshire

Berelowitz S, Firmin C, Edwards G and Gulyurtlu S (2012) *"I thought I was the only one. The only one in the world"*: *The Office of the Children's Commissioner's Inquiry into Child Sexual Exploitation In Gangs and Groups, Interim Report*, London: Office of the Children's Commissioner

Berelowitz S, Clifton J, Firimin C, Gulyurtlu S and Edwards G (2013) *'If only someone had listened'*: *The Office of the Children's Commissioner's Inquiry into Child Sexual Exploitation in Gangs and Groups Final Report*, London: Office of the Children's Commissioner

Brayley H, Cockbain E and Laycock G (2011) 'The value of crime scripting: deconstructing internal child sex trafficking', *Policing: A journal of policy and practice*, 5:2, pp. 132–143

Brown S, Brady G, Franklin A, Bradley L, Kerrigan N and Sealey C (2016). *Child Sexual Abuse and Exploitation: Understanding risk and vulnerability*, London: Early Intervention Foundation

Coleman J, Vellacott J, Solari G, Solari M and Sebba J (2016) *Teenagers in Foster Care: A handbook for foster carers and those that support them*, Oxford: Rees Centre for Research in Fostering and Education

College of Policing (2017) *Authorised Professional Practice: Major investigation and public protection: further investigation*, available at: www.app.college. police.uk/app-content/major-investigation-and-public-protection/child-abuse/ further-investigation/#pre-trial-therapy-and-counselling

Crown Prosecution Service (2013) *Guidelines on Prosecuting Cases of Child Sexual Abuse*, available at: www.cps.gov.uk/legal/a_to_c/child_sexual_abuse/

Department for Education (2017) *Child Sexual Exploitation: Definition and a guide for practitioners, local leaders and decision makers working to protect children from child sexual exploitation*, London: DfE

Department for Education and Home Office (2011) *Safeguarding Children who may have been Trafficked: Practice guidance*, London: DfE and Home Office

Eaton J (2016) *We need to talk about CSE Toolkits*, available at: http:// safeandsoundgroup.org.uk/blog/we-need-to-talk-about-cse-toolkits/

Firmin C and Curtis G (2015) *Practitioner Briefing #1: What is peer-on-peer abuse?*, London: MsUnderstood Partnership

Fox C and Kalkan G (2016) *Barnardo's Survey on Online Grooming*, London: Barnardo's

Gilligan P (2016) Turning it around: what do young women say helps them to move on from child sexual exploitation?, *Child Abuse Review,* 25:2, pp. 115–127

HMIP, HMIC, CQC and Ofsted (2016) *'Time to listen'– a joined up response to child sexual exploitation and missing children,* London: Ofsted

Jay A (2014) *Independent Inquiry into Child Sexual Exploitation in Rotherham 1997–2013,* Rotherham: Rotherham Council

La Valle I and Graham B with Hart D (2016) *Child Sexual Exploitation: Support in children's residential homes,* London: DfE

Marshall K (2014) *CSE in Northern Ireland: Report of the Independent Inquiry conducted by Kathleen Marshall,* Belfast: DH

Nutland C (no date) *The 'Party Lifestyle' Model: The new face of grooming in the UK,* available at: www.safeguardingchildrenea.co.uk/resources/party-lifestyle-model-new-face-grooming-uk

PACE UK (2014) *The Relational Safeguarding Model: Best practice in working with families affected by CSE,* London: PACE UK

PACE UK (no date) *Supporting your Child in Court*, available at: www.paceuk.info/for-parents/advice-centre/if-your-child-gives-evidence-in-court

Perry K (2014) *Rotherham: 'Brazen' sex abusers sent taxis to collect girls from children's home,* London: The Telegraph

Shuker L (2013) *Evaluation of Barnardo's Safe Accommodation Project for Sexually Exploited and Trafficked Young People*, University of Bedfordshire

Shuker L (2015) *Multidimensional Safety for Children in Care Affected by Sexual Exploitation,* available at: www.beds.ac.uk/ic/films

Smith G (2015) *The Protectors' Handbook* (2nd ed), London: CoramBAAF

The Blast Project (2016) *Assessing and Responding to Boys at Risk of CSE,* London: The Blast Project

University of Bedfordshire and NatCen Social Research (2016) *Aycliffe Secure Centre Child Sexual Exploitation Innovation Project Evaluation Summary*, available at: http://springconsortium.com/wp-content/uploads/2016/11/Durham-Aycliffe-Evaluation-Summary-v2.pdf

Vyas S (2015), 'Hackney ex-gangster highlights rise of sexual abuse in gangs', *Hackney Gazette*, 12 February, available at www.hackneygazette.co.uk/news/crime-court/exclusive-hackney-ex-gangster-highlights-rise-of-sexual-abuse-in-gangs-1-3954027

Useful organisations

Barnardo's

The largest provider of CSE support in the UK, with over 40 child sexual exploitation services providing one-to-one support to children and young people who have been exploited. Barnardo's actively identifies and reaches out to young people at risk in the community and its highly skilled professionals provide confidential support in a safe environment. They offer one-to-one counselling, group work and drop-in sessions to help those affected by child sexual exploitation to escape and recover from their abuse. They also support young victims in the criminal justice system.

Its services help to raise awareness of CSE locally, working with schools to deliver preventative education programmes, as well as training professionals and members of community organisations so that they understand what to look out for. Barnardo's also campaigns for legislative change that will help bring abusers to justice, and to improve policy to ensure that children are better protected.

www.barnardos.org.uk

Basis Training and Education

Part of a network of charitable projects with a key focus on CSE and adult sex work. It designs and delivers specialist training on CSE, sexual violence and working with sex workers.

www.basistraining.org.uk

The BLAST Project

Provided various national resources and delivers the UK's longest running, most established male CSE training, all of which address the issues associated with gender inequality in relation to male CSE.

www.mesmac.co.uk/projects/blast

The Lucy Faithfull Foundation (LFF)

The only UK-wide child protection charity dedicated solely to reducing the risk of children being sexually abused. It works with families that have been affected by sexual abuse including adult male and female sexual abusers; young people with inappropriate sexual behaviours; victims of abuse and other family members.

It offers case-specific advice and support, training and development courses and workshops, educational programmes for internet offenders and their families, circles of support and accountability, and internet safety seminars for schools (teachers, parents and children).

LFF established the prevention campaign, Stop it Now! UK and Ireland, which supports adults to protect children through providing information; educating parents, carers and other members of the public; training those who work with children and families; and running a freephone confidential helpline. More information on Stop it Now! UK and Ireland is available on the website.

LFF also runs a website specifically for parents and carers designed to raise awareness of child sexual abuse and provide positive messages about what parents, carers and other adults can do to protect children.

Freephone confidential helpline: 0808 1000 900
Email: help@stopitnow.org.uk
Stop It Now! UK and Ireland: www.stopitnow.org.uk
Parents and carers: www.parentsprotect.co.uk

NSPCC

Works directly with children and families in centres across the UK and campaigns on issues around child sexual abuse. It collaborates with frontline professionals and researchers to find innovative solutions and evaluate what works. It also provides training courses delivered nationwide and online.

www.nspcc.org.uk

National Working Group (formerly The National Working Group for Sexually Exploited Children and Young People)

A UK network of over 12,000 practitioners who disseminate information through their services, to professionals working on CSE and trafficking within the UK. It runs CSE training events and specialist seminars, special interest forums and a monthly members' surgery to discuss enquiries via Skype, FaceTime or conference call. It offers training tools and community awareness resources. It has a resource library and a directory of CSE projects, organisations and services across the UK. It also runs Say Something, a national service that provides young people with a means of reporting CSE through a free, 24/7, anonymous helpline.

National CSE Response Unit, www.nwgnetwork.org

Response unit (for professionals): 0300 303 3032

PACE (Parents Against Child Sexual Exploitation)

The leading national charity working with parents and carers of children who are – or are at risk of being – sexually exploited by perpetrators outside the family. It offers guidance and training to professionals on how CSE affects the whole family.

It provides: national parent telephone support; parent liaison officers; volunteer befriending scheme; parent networking days; an online parents' forum; bespoke training for practitioners; influence in national and local policy; and prevention work and parental awareness. It also has a free online awareness resource on the website and some excellent leaflets, including: *Keeping it Together: A parent's guide to coping with CSE,* and *Working with the Police.*

www.paceuk.info

Safe and Sound

Provides support to children, young people and families in Derby and Derbyshire. It supports young people through the criminal justice system following sexual abuse and works at a national level to support the development of policy and response to the sexual exploitation and trafficking of children and young people. Its training arm, JustWhistle, offers specialist training for practitioners across the UK.

www.safeandsoundgroup.org.uk

The Survivors Trust

An umbrella agency for 135 specialist organisations for support for the impact of rape, sexual violence and childhood sexual abuse throughout the UK and

Ireland. It provides support and networking for member agencies; delivers accredited training; raises awareness about rape and sexual abuse and their effect on survivors, their supporters and society at large; and promotes effective responses to rape and sexual abuse on a local, regional and national level.

www.thesurvivorstrust.org

Scotland's National Action Plan to tackle child sexual exploitation

www.gov.scot/resource/0046/00463120.pdf

Further reading

Information library from PACE UK, including:

- Getting the best service from statutory agencies
- Getting help from the police
- How to gather and log information
- If your child is missing
- Utilising legislation
- Handling disclosure
- Managing online risks
- Living with CSE
- Responding to harassment
- Your child and alcohol and drugs
- CSE and pregnancy
- When boys and young men are sexually exploited
- If your child is over 16 years of age
- If it is unsafe for your child to remain at home
- Disruption tools
- Sex offender disclosure scheme
- If your child gives evidence in court
- Case review panels
- When things go wrong

These can be downloaded from www.paceuk.info/for-parents/advice-centre

Books

Teenagers in Foster Care: A handbook for foster carers and those that support them
John Coleman *et al*, University of Oxford Rees Centre for Research in Fostering and Education. Download from: http://reescentre.education.ox.ac.uk/research/teenagers-in-foster-care/

Foster Care and Social Networking: A guide for social workers and foster carers
Eileen Fursland, 2011, CoramBAAF

The Protectors' Handbook: Reducing the risk of child sexual abuse and helping children recover
Gerrilyn Smith, 2008, CoramBAAF
(This is mainly concerned with child abuse within the family rather than CSE, but could still be useful.)

Online safety websites

Thinkuknow: national education and awareness programme

CEOP's e-safety education site, with a wealth of online safety advice for children and young people, parents and professionals, including videos and other resources and training materials suitable for all age groups.

www.thinkuknow.co.uk

Parentzone

Provides news content and advice for parents, as well as running events and training for schools and professionals who work with children and families. Online magazine, *Digital Parenting*, can also be accessed via the website.

www.parentzone.org.uk

UK Safer Internet Centre

Lots of safety advice and resources, plus a helpline for professionals who have concerns about social networking problems for themselves or the children/young people they work with.

www.saferinternet.org.uk

CEOP: the Child Exploitation and Online Protection Centre

A Government law enforcement agency dedicated to eradicating the sexual abuse of children, CEOP aims to track and bring offenders to justice and to disrupt and deter future offending. It also educates and empowers children, young people, parents, carers and professionals with specialist education on online safety. Cases of suspected grooming and online sexual abuse of children can be reported to CEOP at www.ceop.police.uk or using the CEOP report button at www.thinkuknow.co.uk – the button can also be found on many websites or downloaded to your browser or to a child's Facebook page.

Ofcom

Advice for parents about a range of issues, including using digital devices.

www.ofcom.org.uk

Facebook

Information and resources about safety on Facebook.

www.facebook.com/safety

NSPCC online course

The NSPCC, together with CEOP, has developed an online training course called *Keeping Children Safe Online* for adults who work with children and young people. Updated in 2016, this course will help you to think about the issues that children and young people face online.

It covers:

- how children use the internet and technology
- the risks children take online
- harmful content online
- online radicalisation and extremism
- sharing and sexting
- sexual offending against children online
- bullying online

- supporting parents and carers

- supporting children and young people

- how to make organisations safer places for children to go online.

Each section takes about 20–25 minutes to complete, followed by a series of questions. The course includes: teaching pages; film clips; audio recordings; reflective tasks; interactive learning activities and quizzes.

The course costs £30 per person and takes around 3.5 hours online, working at your own pace.

www.nspcc.org.uk/what-you-can-do/get-expert-training/keeping-children-safe-online-course/

Appendix

The role of the Local Safeguarding Children Board (LSCB)

Planning and commissioning services

LSCBs should ensure that the needs of children and young people who have been or may be sexually exploited, and their families, have been considered when planning and commissioning local services.

Every LSCB is expected to assume that CSE occurs within its area unless there is clear evidence to the contrary. CSE should be considered in local needs assessments and, where it is a significant issue, the LSCB should help ensure it is regarded as a priority by the Children's Trust.

Local activity should include measures to prevent children and young people becoming exploited as well as measures to help young people who are exploited and to take action against perpetrators.

Planning local procedures

LSCBs should ensure that specific local procedures are in place covering CSE, which should set out clearly the respective roles and responsibilities of local agencies and professionals. The strong associations that have been identified between different forms of sexual exploitation, running away from home, child trafficking and substance misuse should also be borne in mind. All agencies with responsibilities for safeguarding and promoting the welfare of children and young people should be involved in drawing up these procedures.

Local areas should continually assess how young people are being groomed for sexual exploitation and make enquiries about the other routes into sexual exploitation taking place in their area. They should amend their intervention approaches to take account of new knowledge as the models of exploitation change over time.

As a minimum, the procedures should specify:

- how to identify signs of sexual exploitation;

- how professionals can seek help and advice on this issue;

- how professionals can and should share information about concerns, appropriately and at the right times, with all relevant agencies in line with the Government's information-sharing guidance;

- the establishment of lead professionals in the key agencies, the routes for referring concerns – preferably through a CSE co-ordinator – and how concerns about sexual exploitation, including those that may arise from use of the Common Assessment Framework, relate to thresholds for referral to statutory agencies;

- how professionals can work together to deliver disruption plans;

- the role of professionals in gathering and preserving the integrity of evidence about perpetrators of sexual exploitation;

- the processes and possible responses for supporting children and young people who have been identified as being at risk of sexual exploitation or are being sexually exploited;

- how to manage situations in conjunction with neighbouring and other local authority areas where children and young people who have been sexually exploited are believed to have lived or temporarily been present or where abusers and coercers have been present;

- how to deal with issues relating to migrant children in situations which make them vulnerable to sexual exploitation;

- how to manage situations of sexual exploitation through the use of technology, such as the internet.

Training

LSCBs should ensure that local safeguarding training includes information about how to identify the warning signs of and vulnerabilities to sexual exploitation, and covers all the issues.

Local training should also help to develop an understanding of how to gather evidence which can be used effectively against abusers. Where sexual exploitation is known to exist locally, LSCBs should ensure that specialist training is available for all key professionals.

Communicating and raising awareness

LSCBs should identify any issues around sexual exploitation, including those arising from the views and experiences of children and young people in their area.

Guidance for the local community on sexual exploitation should include:

- awareness-raising activities focused on young people;
- publicity for sources of help for victims;
- how and where to report concerns about victims and offenders;
- public awareness campaigns more generally;
- monitoring and evaluation of case work.

Monitoring

LSCBs should put in place systems to track and monitor cases of sexual exploitation that come to the attention of local agencies, including schools, colleges and other education organisations; health, the police, social care, housing services; and voluntary and community sector organisations. It would clearly be helpful if LSCBs could share key data with one another and with national organisations to improve the evidence base on sexual exploitation and work to address it.

Adapted from: *Safeguarding Children and Young People from Sexual Exploitation: Supplementary guidance to working together to safeguard children.* DCSF, 2009

PARENTING MATTERS

This unique series provides expert knowledge about a range of children's health conditions, coupled with facts, figures and guidance presented in a straightforward and accessible style. Adopters and foster carers also describe what it is like to parent an affected child, "telling it like it is", sharing their parenting experiences and offering useful advice.

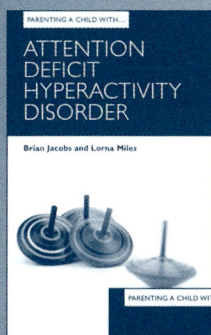

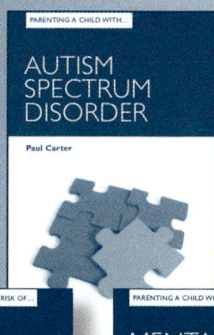

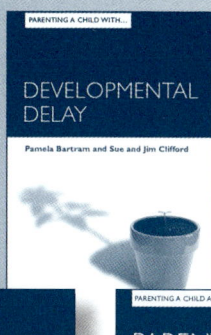

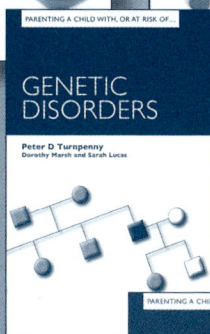

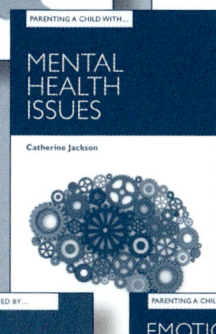

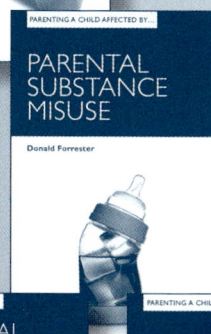

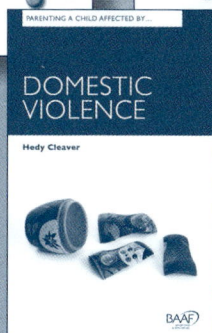

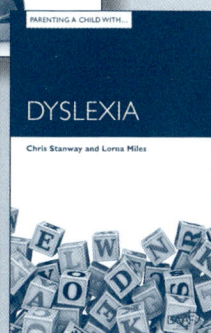

PARENTING A CHILD WITH...
ATTENTION DEFICIT HYPERACTIVITY DISORDER
Brian Jacobs and Lorna Miles

PARENTING A CHILD WITH...
AUTISM SPECTRUM DISORDER
Paul Carter

PARENTING A CHILD WITH...
DEVELOPMENTAL DELAY
Pamela Bartram and Sue and Jim Clifford

PARENTING A CHILD WITH, OR AT RISK OF...
GENETIC DISORDERS
Peter D Turnpenny
Dorothy Marsh and Sarah Lucas

PARENTING A CHILD WITH...
MENTAL HEALTH ISSUES
Catherine Jackson

PARENTING A CHILD AFFECTED BY...
PARENTAL SUBSTANCE MISUSE
Donald Forrester

PARENTING A CHILD AFFECTED BY...
DOMESTIC VIOLENCE
Hedy Cleaver

PARENTING A CHILD WITH...
EMOTIONAL AND BEHAVIOURAL DIFFICULTIES
Dan Hughes

PARENTING A CHILD WITH...
DYSLEXIA
Chris Stanway and Lorna Miles

To find out more visit www.corambaaf.org.uk/bookshop